YOU
POET

LEARN THE ART. SPEAK YOUR TRUTH.
SHARE YOUR VOICE.

HER HEART POETRY's *Rayna Hutchison*
and Samuel Blake

Adams Media

New York   London   Toronto   Sydney   New Delhi

Adams Media
An Imprint of Simon & Schuster, Inc.
57 Littlefield Street
Avon, Massachusetts 02322

First Adams Media trade paperback edition September 2018

ADAMS MEDIA and colophon are trademarks of Simon & Schuster.

For information about special discounts for bulk purchases, please contact Simon & Schuster Special Sales at 1-866-506-1949 or business@simonandschuster.com.

The Simon & Schuster Speakers Bureau can bring authors to your live event. For more information or to book an event contact the Simon & Schuster Speakers Bureau at 1-866-248-3049 or visit our website at www.simonspeakers.com.

Interior design by Katrina Machado
Interior images © Getty Images/GeorgePeters, RichVintage, kertu_ee, lisegagne, David_Sch, puflic_senior, EXTREME-PHOTOGRAPHER, FROGWORKS, tunart, rabbit75_ist, Sabine Hortebusch, Hemera Technologies, Rasoft74, Rohappy, PhotoPepp, Besjunior, rvlsoft; 123RF/Ольга Мелихова, hellena13

Manufactured in the United States of America

10 9 8 7 6 5 4 3 2

Library of Congress Cataloging-in-Publication Data has been applied for.

ISBN 978-1-5072-0834-2
ISBN 978-1-5072-0835-9 (ebook)

CONTENTS

INTRODUCTION

Ink
wells up
and spills forth,
staining my fingers with
poetry.

Do your fingers itch to capture a thought or feeling through words and ink? Have you imagined becoming the next great poet? Whether you are new to poetry or hoping for a fresh perspective; whether you write free verse or rhyme, short poems or long, currently share your work with others, or are still finding the courage to hit the "Post" button, *You/Poet* was written for you. The writing toolbox and creativity-boosting prompts in *You/Poet* are designed to help you, the budding poet, better understand the craft of poetry and improve your writing, guiding you from beneath the leaves and into the sunlight as a full-fledged lyricist ready to share your talent, truth, and voice with the world.

To help you on your creative journey, we have divided *You/Poet* into four parts. In the first part you'll find a brief history of poetry and the voices that shaped the art form we love—from a famous poet like Homer, who provided the foundation for the poetry we read today, to the poetic forms of today: poetry that is short and sharp, and poetry that has jumped off the page and into spoken form. Here we will also help you to uncover the ingredients that make your poetic voice unique—and how to blend them into poems that you can truly be proud of.

Once you've connected with your voice, we'll help you to improve your poetry writing. Part 2 is your guide to key poetry concepts, as well activities that will allow you to practice those concepts. You'll learn the fundamentals of grammar and punctuation, the essentials of every poet's toolbox; word choice and rhyming; meter; and metaphor. Soon you'll be describing this very book through vivid metaphor; is it a vessel cut from wood, moving you through poetry as a ship moves its crew through stormy waters? Or perhaps it is a pirate's tattered map, showing the way to precious treasure (a.k.a. your work—published!). In poetry, the possibilities are endless. Here you'll also work through the basics of editing, so that once you've got the perfect poem written, you don't have to worry about messing up your flawless post with that one stubborn letter that strayed out of place.

In Part 3 you'll be able to put everything you have learned about yourself and poetry together with seventy unique and interactive writing prompts. Sculpt the meaning of a beautiful and uncommon word into a short poem about distance, and ponder the colors and shapes of a photograph, transcribing your thoughts onto the page. Suffering from writer's block? No worries—these exercises will help kick your creativity into gear.

The final part of our creative journey is dedicated exclusively to sharing your poetry. From traditional publishing and poetry competitions, to sharing on social platforms like *Instagram*, *Twitter*, and *Facebook*, you'll discover a complete guide to translating your words—and the emotions within them—onto the digital "page," connecting with other writers, and gaining an online following—everything you need to get your name and work out there! *You/Poet* is your road map for finding your voice and your place in the ever-growing digital poetry community—the incredible journey starts here.

PART 1

A History of Poetry

Many of us have a box stashed away inside our closet: old pictures, journals, and poems written by a younger version of yourself. Isn't it high time you took that thing out again? Shake off the dust and ready your pen, because poetry is flourishing once again—thanks to the digital age we are in! Join the ranks of those who have been writing and regaling poems since we learned to write and regale, and find out how that beautiful heritage pertains to you, a poet residing in the twenty-first century.

Part 1 is where we lay the groundwork for you, a burgeoning poet, as you set out on this creative—possibly rhyming—adventure! You'll learn about the rich history of poetry and how it relates to your personal experience as a writer in the twenty-first century. You'll also discover the first steps on the path toward identifying your own voice as a poet, so that by the time the first chapter is done, you'll feel ready to take on the contemporary world of digital poetry. Let's start!

CHAPTER 1
Poetry 101: An Introduction to Poetry

Someone asks you, "What is poetry?" What do you tell them? More importantly, do you think you can explain it in a way that he or she will understand and appreciate poetry once you're done? Poetry is incredibly difficult to define, because it is something wonderfully different to every person. To one person, poetry is simple nursery rhymes: tales that teach kids to share, take risks, and be nice. To another person, however, poetry reveals something within him- or herself regarding their place in the world: it shows what it means to be honest and vulnerable, tells stories inspiring bravery and risk-taking, and helps us tackle subjects that might otherwise make us uncomfortable. Our reasons for writing, reading, and enjoying poetry are varied, but no matter the cause, poetry's effects remain consistent across the board: it's all about expression. In this chapter, you'll look at poetry through a wide-angle lens to get the big picture. First, you'll read about the history of poetry to understand its origins. After that, you'll learn about poetry's varied uses, and finally, you'll return to the twenty-first century, where you'll see how even the most delicate subject becomes relatable through poetry.

SO CLASSIC!

Millennia have passed since people began exploring the art of expression, and in that time we've experienced major advances in medicine, education, technology, and countless other fields. But there are a rare few wheels that, even after 2,000 years of advancement, simply do not require reinvention. Poetry has definitely seen its share of additions, but the forms and general composition of poetry from ancient days are still in use today. Okay no, we aren't burning our poems into wood or chiseling them into stone—but as far as the basics are concerned, poetry is the same today as it was back when Homer first recounted his epics, *The Iliad* and *The Odyssey*.

The term *epic* might be a little confusing: nowadays *epic* is mostly used to describe something incredible (dinner was epic, an epic fail, or, "Epic wave, brah [*toss a shaka*]!"). However, back when the Greek poet known as Homer was composing his works, people knew epics to be grand tales that told the history (albeit a slightly embellished version) of a region, hero, or legend. If you've ever read Homer's epics, you know how novel-like they are: *The Odyssey* on its own is more than four hundred pages long. It may surprise you, though, to learn that back in Homer's day, epics were usually non-rhyming and recited orally instead of being written. Chew on that for a moment: when was the last time you told a story from memory that was twenty pages long—let alone four hundred?

And Homer wasn't even the first of his kind! Poetry goes back so far that no one knows for sure when the first poem was spoken. It's an art form that has been used by people from all walks of life to entertain, inspire, and teach. Need to learn the alphabet? There's a rhyme for that. Are you feeling bummed out and need some upbeat lyrics to brighten your day? Done. In fact, you would be hard-pressed to find a situation that hasn't been written about in a poem at some point in history, and rightly so! We are deeply expressive, and as society grows and we interact with the world around us, new experiences are created every minute, so it's only fitting that we not only record those events but also appreciate them for the unique insights and realizations they provide.

IF YOU THOUGHT MEMORIZING A HISTORY LESSON WAS TOUGH...

A song contains, on average, 256 words. One English translation of Homer's *The Odyssey* contains 117,319 words: that would be equivalent to memorizing 458 songs!

Take the talented Rupi Kaur, for example. She is one of the most popular poets of this generation, following the self-publication of her collection, *Milk and Honey*, in 2014. Her works touch frequently on uncomfortable, even taboo topics such as violence, loss, abuse, and feminism. Because she expresses her thoughts and feelings on these sensitive subjects through poetry, though, they are easier to relate to and are more open for discussion, learning, and growth. Poetry allows us to take the most difficult aspects of life—the ugliest of the ugly—and turn them into something to laugh about or something to learn from—something we can truly appreciate.

NOW *THAT'S* EPIC!

The oldest written poem on record is an ancient Mesopotamian epic that dates back more than 4,000 years. The *Epic of Gilgamesh* tells the story of Gilgamesh— half-god, half-man—a king who single-handedly pulled together the walls of his city to defend its people from certain death. He definitely set the bar high for Homer's heroes!

Poetry is rich with diversity, complexity, and creativity, which is clearly evident when comparing two people as seemingly opposite as Homer and Rupi Kaur! And now it is time to shift the focus to you (the contemporary poet), your poetry, and everything you can do to put your name up there with the other poetic giants of history. Are you ready?

CHAPTER 2
The Contemporary Poet: Poetry Today

So what does a contemporary poet look like? Chances are you see one every time you look in the mirror! There are, however, some common threads that tie twenty-first-century poets like you together.

The contemporary poet is not only influenced by modern themes, but also by modern technology. Technology plays an important role in how we read and share poetry today, and it is a driver of what is popular in the genre. Where William Shakespeare had the Globe Theatre, the twenty-first-century writer has social media. And while Shakespeare was limited to the page, you—the contemporary poet—are only limited by your access to an Internet connection.

> ### THE CONTEMPORARY POET'S "PEN"
> Use your memo pad or a notepad app on your cell phone to capture poems. OneNote, Simplenote, and GNote are all great apps that can help you to write on the go!

#POETRY

Well-known contemporary poets like Rupi Kaur, Atticus, Lang Leav, and Christopher Poindexter began their careers by posting on the social media platform, *Instagram*. They, along with countless others like them, are leading a renaissance of this time-honored literary form, and based on the hundreds of thousands of poetry accounts and millions of poems shared across multiple digital platforms, it is obvious that #poetryisnotdead.

Technology—specifically social media—is not only shaping how we share and read poetry; it is also shaping contemporary poetic forms. Just as ancient epics and Shakespearean sonnets created influential movements, digital poetry is changing what we write and how we write it. Social media platforms support brevity; in order to make a connection in this fast-paced, easily-distracted world, a poem often needs to be able to be read within minutes, or even seconds. This need for brevity has led to the rise in popularity of micropoetry.

A *micropoem* is simply a short poem of no more than one hundred words and two verses. In the world of digital poetry, if you are looking to grow your followers, length is everything. The most popular poetry accounts on *Instagram* and *Facebook* are the ones that specialize in micropoems, and poetry on *Twitter* is restricted to 280 characters, or the length of a tweet. These poems have their very own genre, known as Twitterature.

The visual nature of these sharing platforms has also sparked the blending of words and art. Contemporary poets have embraced background images and illustrations to enhance their poems, and depict what a poem is describing. The ability to manipulate images using free phone apps means that poets can do this quickly, easily, and without having to pay for expensive software. Poets have also taken to the digital stage and spoken word is becoming increasingly popular.

Modern ideals like individuality and freedom of expression have also influenced poetic structure. Contemporary poets often write in free verse, using modern language and colloquialisms (expressions using informal, conversational style). Instead of the more rigid forms of the past, many poets today use forms of their own making. There is one notable exception: the popularity of micropoetry has resulted in a renaissance of traditional Japanese poem forms such as the haiku, katauta, tanka, and sedoka. The rules of these forms make them a perfect fit for the contemporary micropoem.

THE POWER OF A PEN NAME

If you want to share your poetry, but not your true identity, it is a good idea to use a pen name. A pen name is one that you choose for yourself, and is the "face" of your poetry. This can be very helpful if your work is confrontational or covers traditionally taboo topics.

We also consider the contemporary poet to be fearless! The contemporary poet is unafraid of political topics. Themes that are considered confrontational, such as sexual and physical violence, social justice, mental health, and suicide, are now commonly explored and discussed. Contemporary poets are still writing about the stars in the sky and the beating of the heart, but they are also writing about the ugly and the painful sides of life. Many poets leave a piece of themselves exposed in their poetry. Although traditional themes of nature, relationships, and romance are still common, contemporary poets have been able to use both the anonymity and the community of shared experiences found on the Internet to explore topics that were once off-limits. Poetry today is powerful and challenging. Globally shared connections have given poets a place to be vulnerable in their work. That has meant that more and more, poetry reflects multiple experiences, including those that are painful and dark.

There is no doubt that poetry is not only surviving in the age of social media, it is thriving. Contemporary poets just like you can find a place for your voice and experience in the many multifaceted digital poetry communities available online. Poetry continues to be an important form of modern expression, and just as it has throughout history, it will continue to be an influential part of the creative landscape.

CHAPTER 3
Spoken Word: More Than Pen and Paper

▲▲▲

Long before the inception of pen and paper, societies were using spoken histories and stories as a way to share culture and beliefs. From the ancient Greeks to the East African Kikuyu to the Māori of New Zealand—and many other cultures in between—oral traditions have allowed for expression and connection since the beginning of language. Contemporary spoken word is no different: it is poetry spoken to create a connection between speaker and listener. As poet laureate Robert Pinsky once said, "The medium of poetry is not words, the medium of poetry is not lines—it is the motion of air inside the human body, coming out through the chest and the voice box and through the mouth to shape sounds that have meaning. It's bodily." Spoken word poetry gives life to this notion, in that poetry only becomes truly alive when it is spoken.

WHAT IS SPOKEN WORD EXACTLY?

Spoken word is performance poetry. In essence, the poet reads a piece of poetry aloud, paying attention to word selection and word interplay, inflection, intonation, and the expression of meaning and emotion through voice. Spoken word poems are written just like any other poem. However, the poet must carefully consider how words will flow together and how they will sound when heard, rather than just being read. Understanding poetic devices like rhyme and meter is important, as they are often used in spoken word, and can enhance or sink a performance.

Unlike poems that are bound to a page, spoken word poems are often accompanied by music. They also have an element of acting in their delivery and spoken word poets need to consider the tone of their voice, the look on their faces, and the use of action and gestures to create a connection between the listener and the poem.

GIVING VOICE TO THE VOICELESS

What makes contemporary spoken word more exciting is that it has roots in the social action movements of the 1960s and 1970s. It is believed that spoken word originated from the coffee house–dwelling beat poets of the 1960s. The form evolved during the Harlem Renaissance and the Civil Rights movement and it is widely understood that notable speeches, such as "I Have a Dream" by Dr. Martin Luther King Jr., have influenced spoken word culture. Contemporary spoken word saw its own renaissance with the rise of the poetry slam in the 1990s, drawing on hip-hop and rap as sources of inspiration.

The form truly became mainstream when Russell Simmons created the TV series *Def Poetry Jam*, which aired 2002–2007. This spoken word television series featured poetry performances by both well-known and up-and-coming poets.

WHAT IS SLAM POETRY?

Slam poetry is a type of performance poetry that uses techniques such as rhyming, intonation, hyperbole, and body language to express intense emotions and personal experiences. Poetry slams involve a panel of judges and a public audience.

The tradition of activism through spoken word is still carrying on today and has become a global phenomenon.

Spoken word is commonly used as a vehicle to talk to the disenfranchised and the bullied, to the struggles of women and people of color, and to protest against political views and war. Spoken word performances are now commonplace in the United States, France, the United Kingdom, many parts of Africa, and as far afield as Australia and New Zealand.

POETIC ACTIVISM IN ACTION

Actress Ashley Judd's heartfelt reading of the poem "Nasty Woman," written by nineteen-year-old poet Nina Donovan, at the 2017 Women's March on Washington is one example of the way in which contemporary poetry and activism intersects.

SPOKEN WORD ON THE DIGITAL STAGE

Today, this unique form of expression is helping poets like you breathe life into their words with energetic performances that can be watched and enjoyed online at the click of a button. There are literally thousands of spoken word performances available on *YouTube*, covering diverse topics from identity politics to everyday and extraordinary emotional experiences. The ease of being able to record spoken word poetry in the comfort of our own homes also means that stage fright is no longer a barrier to sharing, and platforms such as *Instagram*, *Facebook*, and, of course, *YouTube*, have given poets everywhere the chance to be seen and heard without leaving their bedrooms.

SET IT TO MUSIC!

Spoken word poets often use background music to accentuate meaning and create impact. Speaking in time with the right piece of music creates flow and dynamism, and can help set the mood of the poem.

SPOKEN WORD IRL

The growing popularity of this form also means that enjoying and participating in spoken word events, or slams, is becoming much easier. In cities all over the world, spoken word nights and clubs that focus on spoken word performances are more and more common. You can find a place to check out performances and showcase your own spoken word poetry on national poetry society websites, such as WellVersedInk.org. Spoken word clubs are also becoming commonplace at high schools and universities. You can learn more by contacting a school representative. Attending slams or group workshops gives you the chance to see spoken word in real life, and to practice the art in a safe and inclusive environment—no matter your experience level.

Love the idea of becoming a spoken word poet? If this form has *spoken* to you it's likely that performing is one element of your creative identity. Even if spoken word poetry doesn't sound like your calling, take note of what does speak to you as you progress through this book, and remember to explore and nurture those passions as part of your poetic voice. Fortunately, we are going to help you find your voice in the next chapter!

CHAPTER 4
Why We Write:
Finding Your Voice

What is your reason for writing? You've always had words whirling around inside your head, searching frantically for the exit to your fingers, but without some kind of motivation, they'd never make it. So what's the point? What's *your* point? In this chapter, you'll identify your own underlying reason for writing, first by exploring some of the classic reasons why writers of yesterday and today chose poetry as their main form of expression. *Why* you write will greatly affect the type of audience that will be listening, and once you know who you're trying to reach, finding your voice is much easier. Everything from the words you choose to the way you decide to string them together plays a role in making your voice heard by that audience. Don't know what your voice sounds like, or if you've even found your voice yet? No worries! We'll go over that too.

WHAT IS POETRY TO YOU?
"For me poetry is the beauty that blooms from pain, the smile in laughter, an energy unleashed…it's in everything; a subtle glance, a loud bang, an autumn breeze." —Nikkeya B.

NEXT STOP: PURPOSE

As with any journey, becoming a better poet requires an understanding of your destination. Before sitting down to write, have you asked yourself, "Where am I going with this? What am I trying to say?" Most poetry can be divided into two "destinations": poems written to express a feeling, and poems written to make a connection with the reader. Both destinations can lead a poet to success, be it wealth, fame, or simply having an emotional outlet, but while they both are wondrous in their own right, the destination you choose will greatly affect the poetry you write.

BE THE MIRROR: REFLECT

Maybe you're the poet who writes to express emotions, many and varied as they are. You may be communicating the pain you feel from losing someone close to you, or the overwhelming joy of finding—at long last!—true and genuine love, but either way, what truly matters is that you are able to, first, put your thoughts and emotions into words and, second, put them onto paper (or a word document on the computer). If you write this way, then your poetry is the *reflective* type: in other words, the emotions of the poem are experienced *by* you and *for* you. It really doesn't matter whether or not others approve of the writing: you have expressed what you set out to express, so mission accomplished!

Reflective poetry is and always has been an incredibly important form of writing. For many it can act as a sort of therapy that helps them to work out complicated emotions and thought processes. Have you ever written a poem as a means of letting go of certain feelings or ideas (e.g., a broken heart or an unhealthy desire)? Even relatively commonplace events like experiencing something for the first time can be easier to handle and work out with the aid of poetry, so for you and other like-minded writers, the ink on your paper may as well be your blood, because it's every bit a part of you as your hands, eyes, and toes. It is poetry that truly comes from the heart.

JUST BE YOURSELF!

Reflective writing isn't bound to the typical rules of grammar. It's more personalized, so if you want to capitalize every other letter, do it! Want to type your letters backwards so that people can relate to a poet with dyslexia? Awesome! Be you, and be proud, you reflective poet you.

BE THE LOOKING GLASS: OBSERVE

If, on the other hand, your writing aims to connect with and otherwise engage your readers (inspiring thoughts and emotions within them regardless of their different positions in life), then your writing is considered *observational*. With observational poetry, the writer's goal is to stir a specific emotion or thought within the reader based on an experience or observation. Even though the reader may not have experienced the same situation in their own life, a well-written observational poem can make the reader feel as though they have. Subjects for this style of writing are incredibly diverse, often touching on global experiences or detailing cultural and societal issues. These poems frequently address those life topics that would be labeled "taboo" in normal social settings. Maybe you've been abused in the past, so as a means of teaching others about the fear you now deal with on a daily basis, you could write a poem describing the event. Did that presidential election not go the way you were hoping it would? Writing an observational poem can be a great way of showing others exactly how much change is needed.

One of the best parts of observational poetry, though, is the freedom we have to experience what would normally be outside of our capability—for example, a grown man can write about what growing up without a father would be like, or a deaf woman can write about what she imagines her husband's voice sounds like. These poems aren't written from direct experience, but because of the ability of poetry to create empathy in its readers, the writer can still evoke very specific and powerful emotions in his or her audience.

BE PRESENT IN THE MOMENT
To practice observational and reflective poetry, sit down outside for five minutes and take in your surroundings. Are there any particular smells that reach your nose? Any colors or activities that catch your eye? When you close your eyes, do you notice anything different? Afterward, spend ten minutes writing about how you feel presently, and then spend another ten minutes writing something that would bring out those emotions in your reader. Good luck!

Thankfully, no one has ever written into law that all poets must be either A or B, so if you want to write an observational poem one minute and a reflective poem the next, by all means get funky with it. In general though, most poets begin their journey with observational poetry—after all, life is constantly happening all around us, and as writers, we must be adept at converting our observations of life into words. Now the questions that remain are: "How do I pick my words?" "How do I know what to write so that I get my point across to the greatest number of people?" Answering these questions, while not easy, will definitely aid you in discovering your voice.

FINDING YOUR VOICE

"By sharing my words I prove to myself that my words matter, that my voice matters, that I will live on, somewhere, in someone's mind and heart."
—Kati M.

Roughly one quarter of the quality of your work can be attributed to your *voice*: the characteristic that communicates some truth about yourself as an individual, as part of a group, or as something in between. The concept sounds simple enough, but many writers, even those who have produced several publications, still don't know their own voice. Your voice as a writer isn't something that can be put on a timeline like a publisher's deadline. In fact, most will stumble upon it when their hands are too cramped to write another word. Your voice is your passions, your anxieties, and your personality, which comes through in certain phrases but holds back in others;

your voice is what remains of you in the written words after they have left your fingers.

Unfortunately, your voice doesn't come with a "how to find me" guide, and your preferred GPS app will be just as useless in the search. The reason you won't find a "how to" book is the same reason why searching the Internet won't help: it simply takes time. That's right, friend: all you have to do to find your voice is keep the words flowing. Okay yes, of course knowing the ins and outs of grammar, expanding your vocabulary, and utilizing all of the free time you can get will go a *long* way toward helping you discover and define your voice as a poet, but when all is said and done, your voice will be most apparent when your comfort with the written word is obvious. And how do you get comfortable with writing? By picking up your pen.

MAKE THIS YOUR MANTRA
When seeking your voice, consider, "When friends and family read my work, do they hear my voice as they read, or do they hear their own voice? Can anyone read my unsigned work and still know that the writing is mine? Can strangers discern insights of my character from my writing?"

A quick word of warning now that you know time is the crucial factor in finding your voice: do not rush yourself! Take your time and understand that your goal—first and foremost—is simply to enjoy the act of writing. Allow your personality and love for writing to naturally guide your practices and skills surrounding the craft.

ONLINE WRITING CHALLENGES

An important part of discovering your voice through practice is determining what works best for you. Many writers find value in participating in daily writing challenges hosted by different social network communities, such as *Her Heart Poetry*, the Round Table Challenge, and *Artlixir Poetry*. These communities excel in challenging their members with vocabulary prompts, imagery challenges, and different poetic forms on a regular basis. Online writing challenges are particularly beneficial to growing poets, because they create writing opportunities while also providing a place where other artists' works can be read, allowing you to both expand your current skill set and see how others are approaching the same idea. Other writers decide to pass on the daily challenges and instead challenge themselves—you know you best, after all. These writers tend to be very hit-or-miss with readers, because they can come across as less focused and "off the beaten path," but they also tend to be the writers who set trends instead of following them, and create poetic forms instead of depending on them.

THAT'S NOT RUBBISH!

Never throw away your old writing. Reading through old work can help you to understand the areas where your writing needs to improve without the embarrassment of putting that work out for the world to judge. Knowing where you've come from is just as important as knowing where you're headed.

Remember, too, that just like you, your voice will likely change with time. Even if you found your voice at an uncommonly young age, it is highly unlikely that, twenty or so years later, you're still writing about the same ideas. Even if there are still some common themes between then and now, surely you're no longer communicating in the same way. Reading through that old, forgotten work can be very beneficial, though, and it's a practice many accomplished writers utilize. If you have any old journals or poetry, try reading through them a couple times a year, paying attention to what has changed. How has your writing improved? Has it gotten worse in any way? What does your old writing have in common with your current writing? Ask yourself every question you can when reading through your previous works, because with every answer, you'll be that much closer to discovering your voice.

Before we move on to the techniques and tools for writing poetry, let's do a quick recap: you read up on a brief history of poetry and saw how concepts formed ages ago still influence writing today; you learned the differences between the two "destinations" of poetry and how they factor into your personalized writing style; and you explored the poet's voice and methods you can practice to get more comfortable with written words. It's been a busy section, to be sure, but now it's time to get into the nitty-gritty of the craft!

PART 2

The Craft of Poetry

What is a pianist without his piano, or a pilot without her plane? Pencil and paper aside, many of your tools may not be the kind you can hold in your hand or use to cross oceans, but whether you're a novelist, an ink-bound poet, or a speaker-extraordinaire, things like grammar, vocabulary, punctuation, and imagery are devices you'll need to get where you want to go. Granted, these tools may be fluid in later poetic use, but any practitioner of language should be familiar with them, and constantly working to add new instruments to his or her tool-box. Think of Part 2 as your local hardware store—for poets!

CHAPTER 5
Using Your Poetic Tools: Themes, Images, Metaphors, Similes, and Punctuation

Toolboxes come in various shapes, sizes, and colors, but most of them have multiple compartments for storing tools according to their function, size, and frequency of use, and a poet's toolbox is no different! Some tools, like themes and imagery, aren't needed for every job, so you can safely store them in a removable shelf, but others—punctuation, metaphors, and similes—you will need for each piece of writing you compose, even if you are a spoken word poet. In poetry, how you use your tools is somewhat open to interpretation, but the fact remains that if you don't understand what's in your toolbox, you'll never be able to get the job done properly.

In this chapter, you're not going to just look inside the poet's toolbox: you're going to learn how each tool works and how you can use them to add depth and character to your poetry. We'll cover the indispensable tools that you'll take to every job—punctuation, metaphors, and similes—and we'll also take a look at how other items (e.g., imagery and themes), while not necessary for each piece you write, could take your poetry to the next level. You'll also be able to see that your toolbox still has room for one more tool...or twenty! Hopefully by the time this chapter is finished, you'll feel much more confident and capable of composing your very own masterpiece.

PUNCTUATION

As a poet, punctuation is one of the most important tools at your disposal, regardless of whether you are confined to ink and paper, a digital format, or the spoken word. Every thought you try to communicate, every image you want to paint in the mind of your readers, and every emotion you attempt to convey, will require you to understand and utilize punctuation. Unfortunately, so many types of punctuation exist in the world that there's no way we'll be able to look at each of them up close, but we will certainly check out the main poetry "fasteners" at our disposal!

COMMAS

Contrary to popular belief, a comma is not punctuation used to indicate where you—reader or writer—should pause or breathe in a statement. Many, *many* would-be poets lose their audience to too many unnecessary commas, or worse, no commas or punctuation whatsoever (insert choking sounds). The truth is, commas are very simple to use properly! If you need to separate the parts of a sentence, create a list, or denote large numerical values, use a comma. If your goal is to create space between certain words or syllables for emphasis, though, either omit the comma (possibly for a period instead), or only use it for personal reference in the event that you're reading your work aloud.

In the following list you'll find common examples for using commas appropriately. Familiarize yourself with them, because if punctuation is a tool you're going to need in every job, then commas are undoubtedly the grease you'll need to keep your writing working efficiently.

- **Between sections of a compound statement:** "I think, therefore I am." "I think" and "I am" are both complete statements, and "therefore" is the conjunction connecting the two, so a comma before the conjunction is correct.
- **Separating items in a list:** "Broken, blinded, scarred, and lost, my torment lingers on." Whether it's a list of adjectives describing the sentence's subject, or a list of nouns, each word should be separated by a comma—even after "scarred."
- **Offsetting an introductory phrase:** "Not prone to wander, her love remained locked up inside." "Not prone to wander" is a statement used to further describe "her love," and since it comes before the subject as an introduction of sorts, a comma is used to separate the two parts.

Most of us know what a comma is, and even though we'll accidentally include one where it's not required from time to time, a rogue comma will rarely throw off an entire piece. What *does* have that potential, however, is its misunderstood stepbrother, the semicolon.

SEMICOLONS

If your toolbox has been sitting on a shelf in the garage for ages, you might go through it one day and pull out a strange-looking tool that is a complete mystery to you. Let's call this tool the semicolon. Across the board, fewer writers know how to use the semicolon than any other element of punctuation in the English language. Thankfully, semicolons are not all that difficult to understand! They are primarily used to separate two related but independent statements not joined by a conjunction and can also be used in place of a comma for lists wherein the list items are more detailed or already contain commas. That's quite a bit to take in, so let's mull over a couple of examples:

"The light shone upon me; my heart was filled."

In this first example, we have two statements that can stand alone. In poetry, we frequently use semicolons to draw more obvious connections between two independent thoughts. Thanks to the semicolon in this example, we know that the author's heart was filled *because* the light shone upon him. Be careful to note that when you're using a semicolon this way, the conjunction that would've been there is dropped (e.g., "The light shone upon me, *and* my heart was filled.").

"I know not where my hot-blooded, adventurous heart will roam; when the beast inside will awaken, ravenous and crazed; whence its melodious, siren-song calls; but I do know, that I will never cease to pursue its every desire."

This second example uses the semicolon to replace commas that would normally separate items in the list. Since the items in this list are more descriptive though, and because they already contain commas themselves, semicolons replace the item-separating commas to prevent confusion. Also note that when using a semicolon is this situation, the conjunction "but" is still necessary, so the semicolon doesn't replace it.

The semicolon has other functions, too, but these two main uses are what you will come across most frequently. If you're still having trouble trying to decide whether or not you should use a semicolon, just remember: except in complex lists, a semicolon is, more or less, exactly what it looks like—a fancy nail pinning together two related statements. Don't forget to remove the conjunction before hammering it into place, and you're all set!

PRACTICE DOESN'T MAKE PERFECT

Practice makes *permanent*, not perfect. If you're practicing the use of semicolons incorrectly, all you're doing is teaching your brain, "This is how it's done," when in reality, it's not. Make sure you fully understand the uses of every type of punctuation before you really dive into practice time.

(FULL-FLEDGED) COLONS

A colon looks just as strange as its second cousin, the semicolon, but fear not—it is a bit easier to master. Colons are used to explain or illustrate the previous phrase. If you're trying to say, "Here's what I mean," or "That is to say," then the colon is the tool for you. Here is an example:

> Threshing floors loose grains of rice,
> Falling twixt my fingers twice,
> In my head, Mother's advice:
> Work hard to earn your wage!

Undoubtedly, this author's mother had more advice to give her child than simply, "Work hard," but at least you can see how the colon is used correctly within poetry. As the author is working, he's thinking about his mother's advice, *that is to say*, "Work hard to earn your wage!" Pretty cool how that works, isn't it?

Colons can also be used to denote the beginning of a list. Where *Instagram* and the world of micropoetry are concerned, lists aren't going to be an incredibly common occurrence (since that would sort of contradict the *micro* aspect of the poem), but it's still good to know that you have the option. Following is an example of poetry wherein the author uses a colon to start a list of items. Note that the items in the list can all be directly tied back to the statement preceding the colon: if you ever write a colon-formed list where this isn't the case, then the colon has been misused.

> The toils of this world are great,
> But not so countless as the joys she's made:
> The salty kiss of ocean's ebbing tide,
> The midnight crow who cackles at passersby,
> That longing hung upon your scarlet lips,
> and back arching softly just at the hip.

As you can see, each item in the list, though a separate poetic thought, can be directly linked to the line before the colon, "But not so countless as the joys she's made." Each item in the list details a specific joy as experienced by the writer, so you can tell that the colon has been used correctly.

So now that you've stocked up on some of the tool-belt basics, let's take a look at how you can go from being "some guy with a hammer and nails" to "a master craftsman with a plan." After all, it's not enough to simply own the tools: you have to pick them up and create something beautiful to be called a true master.

SIMILES

The second most important tool at our disposal is the simile. A simile is a comparison of one object to another by way of the words "like" and "as." Similes allow us to take a common, mundane object and breathe new life into it by comparing it to another, more fascinating and vivid object.

> ### GIVE SIMILES A TRY!
> Let's use this book as an example! Take a minute, and try describing this book with similes so that it's more exciting to read about, and don't hold back! Be as outlandish as you want! Write down your best comparisons, and let someone you trust read them. Did the comparisons come across like you intended?

Being the artistic observers that they are, poets commonly use similes in their writing to help paint specific pictures in the reader's mind, or to create a means of comprehending more difficult subjects like violence and depression—issues that not everyone experiences or understands. Here is an example:

> Looking to the glitt'ring sky
> I felt my soul take flight,
> Wings spread wide like black magpie
> Take off toward starlight.

Adjectives like "glitt'ring" play their part in bringing life to your poetry, but similes are where the truest artistry takes place. By comparing the wings of his soul to those of the black magpie (a jet-black bird with a bright, white chest), the poet makes sure that every reader will have a clearer image of the poet's soul in their mind, and with any luck, that image will more closely match the poet's intent.

Here's the catch: similes are so common in poetry, both ancient and modern, that overusing this tool or using it in the same way every time can leave your poetry feeling shallow and repetitive. We'll touch on this more in the next chapter, but for now just understand that, as a budding poet, you will have to put a great deal of thought into your similes if you want them to be effective.

METAPHORS

Metaphors are incredibly similar to similes (you might even say *like* similes), but where similes compare two objects, metaphors directly equate them by means of either the word "is" or "are." Many young poets struggle with metaphors for a couple of reasons: one, it's human nature to draw comparisons between similar things, so similes are kind of like our human default setting; and two, the sound of metaphorical statements can leave a line of poetry feeling archaic and unclear, especially if the two objects being equated are particularly abstract. Here's an example to help clear up any confusion:

PART 2: THE CRAFT OF POETRY

War is a broken vase,
Capable of being filled,
Unable to sustain.

In the example, the author uses a metaphorical statement to directly equate war with a broken piece of pottery. To understand why metaphors can be difficult to use, only read the first line. The meaning of the metaphor isn't very clear, is it? What you imagine when you think of "a broken vase" might be completely different than what the next reader imagines, so it's important that both your metaphors and similes are well thought out. Because the author continues his poem by explaining the meaning behind his metaphor, his readers are on the same page, and the imagery is understood.

METAPHOR PRACTICE TIME!

You've practiced using similes to describe this book, now let's practice the same routine using metaphors. A little more complicated, isn't it? Don't get discouraged. Even the most veteran poets struggle with finding a solid metaphor. The more you challenge yourself with these critical thinking practices, the easier it will be to think them up on the fly.

Fully equipped with a working understanding of similes and metaphors, you may be thinking, "Great, but I still only have a bunch of words on paper. How do I really make them pop when I don't actually *know* the people who are reading them?" Good question! In the next section, you'll explore how your poetry can use themes and images to pull in readers.

IMAGES AND THEMES

Now that we've rummaged through our toolboxes a little more and polished a couple of the tools we'll never leave home without, you may be thinking, "Well what good is a hammer without nails? What use have I for a drill if I have no screws?" Where carpenters deal with nails and masons work with mortar, our essential fasteners as poets of the twenty-first century are images and themes. What's the best part about these tools? You can bring them out more frequently with your essentials, or keep them in the toolbox until you're ready to use them a bit more sporadically: the choice is yours.

That being said, you may consider the modern world of digital media and social networking as you write. The average attention span for most people is limited to somewhere between a measly two and twenty minutes, and especially where *Instagram*—a visually dominated platform—is concerned, if you can't hook someone into your writing within the first couple lines, you're probably not going to hook them at all. Thankfully, we artsy types have the tools to give us an edge.

IMAGES

Sometimes an actual image—a simple outline, a single flower petal, or even just a background image—is all you need to drive home the picture you're painting with your poetry. If you've ever heard the saying, "A picture is worth a thousand words," then just imagine what can be done with a picture *and* a few carefully chosen words. As a poet, you have the good fortune of being able to take a single moment in time (e.g., a picture or part of a picture) and work it into an interpretation of your own choosing. You can take the picture of a rose, for example, and instead of talking about the love it represents or the pain caused by its thorns (so cliché and boring!), you can focus solely on its scarlet petals and create vivid imagery in the minds of your readers that way. Here is an example poem:

> Dressed in scarlet thick as wool
> Across her chest cascades,
> Desire rising in me full,
> Though confidence still fades.

The imagery crafted by your words becomes more clearly illustrated with your image of the rose, because it provides the same visual focus for every reader. Thanks to hashtags, you can also attract potential readers seeking both poetry *and* pretty flowers: #rose #poetsofinstagram.

As you strive for greatness, eventually you're going to reach a point where you're producing a lot of pieces of writing, and that's when you can really make your work shine by focusing on different themes.

THEMES

A theme is essentially a collection of works that all focus on the same general concept. Sticking with the rose image, you could draft a series of poems in which each focuses on a different part of the flower: one for its color, one for its scent, one for its nature, and one for how it's spent. By creating a theme, you give your audience more unique insights into a certain subject; you challenge yourself to think outside the box, thereby continuing your growth as a poet; and you create more opportunities to increase your viewership. That makes three birds with one stone—not too shabby!

Cheesy gimmicks about toolboxes and birds aside, you will not succeed as a poet without a basic understanding of the concepts we have gone over in this chapter. And these facets are barely the tip of the iceberg! If you really want your poetry to flourish, you've got a bit more work to do, and thanks to *You/Poet*, you now have the tools to get started. The next chapter will explore the importance of word choice in your work.

CHAPTER 6
Word Choice: Why Your Words Matter

You've seen the term *wordsmith* once or twice before while perusing the many lists of poets available to read online. To think of a writer pounding away at white-hot letters fresh from the furnace is a strange notion, but it's not as far from reality as many would believe. Think about it: if you were going into battle and needed a weapon, you wouldn't ask a blacksmith to forge one out of plastic, right? No way! You'd want a weapon of steel or perhaps even magic! You can understand then why the words poets choose are so important: piecing letters and words together to create coherent and artistic pieces of writing isn't a simple task. By starting out with the best materials possible, you can find the edge you need to emerge victorious.

DID YOU REMEMBER YOUR VOICE?

Maybe you've been devouring poetry and novels since you could read, building your vocabulary word by word. Then again, you could be a young student with dyslexia, and because reading is the source of your greatest frustrations, you only know enough vocabulary to scrape by. Chances are you fall somewhere in between, but wherever you stand, as a poet, your words are your greatest tool. Without a healthy stock of vocabulary to choose from, your poetry can quickly become redundant. Vocabulary is sort of like a screwdriver to any contractor: each looks and feels pretty similar, but only the right one will get the job done right. In this chapter, you'll learn the guidelines for picking out the best words to get the "job" done right, but before we dive in, a disclaimer: though you should be constantly adding to your repertoire, you will be served best by the words that naturally fit your voice.

If you recall, in Chapter 4 we discussed the poet's voice—how your thoughts and emotions are "heard," or interpreted, by your readers. Ideally, your voice should be heard when anyone is reciting or reading your words, because your writing is a reflection of your habits, personality, beliefs, and so on. Using words that are outside the established realm of "your voice" is sort of like gluing a rubber, squeaky clownnose onto your face. Once that bright, red nose of an awkward word choice is posted online, everyone will see it, and nothing you do can stop its incessant squeaking. Don't misunderstand: no one is saying, for example, that a ten-year-old writer is never allowed to use the word *contemplating*, because it doesn't fit his or her young voice. A writer is allowed to use any words he or she wants, but doing so is a risk that may result in confusing long-time readers and losing their loyalty. Before you try out completely new and different words, work on coming up with creative ways to reuse and reinvent the words you already know and are comfortable with.

Now that the disclaimer is out of the way, understand that you're still an artist, and as such, you are prone to interpreting everything in unique and creative ways, so if being the poet who picks random words to paint metaphorical masterpieces around the chaos is crucial to your voice, then by all means, play in the pandemonium until you can't tell your pinks from your purples.

SPEAK, *THEN* SPELL

Before you start using new words in your published works, practice them in private until you're sick of them. Plug a new word into your Internet search engine and take notes on how others are using it. Then try practicing using it in day-to-day conversations. As you become increasingly accustomed to its use, your writing will more accurately reflect your comfort with it.

On a smaller scale, perhaps you're just growing tired of using the same word combinations and illustration techniques. At that point, feel free to take out a thesaurus and look up synonyms for the words you use most frequently. *WAIT!* This is the point where you might feel tempted to replace your typical word choice with one of the synonyms you just found, but if poetry ever had a cardinal sin, you would be committing it. Please understand that a thesaurus is just one half of a complete set of tools: the dictionary is still missing. Before you ever plug a synonym into your poetry, you should know that word backwards and forwards: know all of its forms, its tenses, and each definition it may have. Sometimes a synonym has other, better known meanings, so sticking it in your poem to make it sound less juvenile or more sophisticated can actually have the opposite effect. Remember that patience is the name of the game in poetry. If you're trying to speed things up (as with a thesaurus), you're just going to wind up covered from head to toe in obnoxious, squeaking clown noses.

As long as you continue building your vocabulary using these methods, you will encounter far fewer instances where word choice sticks out unfavorably in your poetry. As we've discovered, the words we choose have a dramatic effect beyond the page. And it doesn't end there!

AS POETS, WE ARE OUR WORDS

Have you ever heard an interview with Shel Silverstein? Do you even know what Dr. Seuss looks like? No? Not surprising. Start rattling off their poetry, though, and most people could identify the author almost immediately, right? That's because what kind of person you are doesn't have much bearing on the fact that, as a poet, you are your words. If you want to become a superstar in the world of poetry, chances are that people will barely know your face at all, let alone what you sound like or wear, or how you spend a lazy, rainy Sunday. They will know your words through and through, however, and that's why it's so important to practice your craft.

HELPING THE HAND CATCH UP TO THE HEART

One of the most useful practices for poets young and old is to routinely write out the words you say *as you speak them*. Cut out all formalities of grammar, sentence structure, and vocabulary, and simply write—word for word—whatever comes out of your mouth. Save the writings, and once you've collected a few, compare them. Over time, this practice will help you identify common speech patterns, word redundancies, and all the little quirks that give personality to your voice. It may feel strange at first, but continuing this practice allows you to process your observations faster, more fluidly translate your thoughts into written words, and create smoother and more understandable transitions between one idea and another. This, in turn, benefits your readers, because they can follow along with your writing easier, thereby winning you a larger audience. Sure, it's going to take a little more time out of your day, but if it's making your writing better, then it's time well spent.

FEEDBACK HELPS THE READ-BACK

One of the most important and beneficial practices in poetry is keeping yourself open to feedback. Your audience is full of new perspectives and ideas that you might never dream up yourself. The more open-minded you are, the faster your writing will improve. Just remember that the choice is yours to accept advice or leave it behind.

However, reaching superstar status requires more practice than just scribbling a three-lined poem or two throughout the week. Eventually, you're going to look around your writing space and find notebook after notebook filled with thoughts and ideas that are nowhere near completion; half-formed rhymes scratched onto Post-its that litter every wall of your house; and a handful of completed works that you have deemed "worthy enough" to actually make it to a public forum. That's perfectly okay though, because one, if you're doing everything we've been talking about, that means you have mountains of material to work with and turn into future masterpieces; and two, you're a poet, and as such, your only "job" is to write whatever feels right to you—not others. Your entire focus should be on enjoying the process and improving your skills in the meantime; if your focus is anywhere else, then you're missing the point. Who you are and what you have to say with your poetry is infinitely more important than whether or not people *like* what you've said.

YOUR WORDS SHAPE HISTORY

Believe it or not, your words are important for reasons outside of the worlds of social media, publishing, and stardom: your words are a part of history. Maybe you've heard the adage, "History is written by the winners," and that's true to some extent: the information that goes into history books and is taught in school is usually written by the people who won the war or otherwise emerged as the dominant species. Make no mistake, however, that history is rarely remembered for the History 101 textbooks bought at the start of term and sold by the end of it: history is known by the people who lived it and recorded their experiences.

This is, perhaps, the most exciting aspect of poetry. Consider for a moment that *Instagram* has more than ninety million monthly users. Even if we assume that only one percent of those accounts are strictly creative writing accounts, that's still 900,000 people across the world who are recording their thoughts, emotions, and experiences in life every month. We're talking about almost one million individualized firsthand accounts of politics, war, economics, social hierarchy, education, and all the other facets that make life the beautiful, frustrating, incredible, and confusing mess it is.

> ## LET IT REST
> As a poet, you are deeply rooted in personal experience and emotion, and you may end up communicating ideas you hadn't intended. Similar to how you should let your work breathe before editing, let it also rest after completion. That way you can look at it with fresh eyes before sending it out into the world.

It's true, we can't exactly write poems today from the 20/20 vision of the future: time machines are unfortunately still a thing of fantasy. Did Emily Dickinson spend all of her time writing in isolation because she knew that, after she died, her works would be cherished for the iconic time-period pieces they are? No. Was William Shakespeare tormented by the stress of knowing that his poetry would essentially shape the field of creative writing for not only his generation, but for future generations? Not likely. The fact remains, though, that the works of these two poets characterized and helped to define the history of our human race, even in their highly artistic forms. It stands to reason, then, that you could very well be the next Dickinson or Shakespeare! That doesn't mean you need to start writing tales of happiness and rainbows, or of woe and sorrow all day long, though. Write whatever you usually write, but write it with the understanding that you have a place in this big world, and even your voice, as insignificant as it may seem, can carry and echo, and it might eventually reach every eye and every ear that roams the land.

WRITING: YOUR DUTY?

Many, many people think of writing as a daunting and downright intimidating task. Asking certain people to translate the thoughts in their head and emotions in their heart into words that other people can read, process, internalize, and respond to, might as well be like asking a duck to grow antennae. If, though, you have that insatiable itch to put pen to paper, then believe it or not, it's your job to do so.

YOU'RE A WRITER
If writing is your natural response to life's experiences, then write, because you are a writer. If you have to force yourself to write frequently, but still love the process, you too are a writer. Absolutely *anyone* can be a writer as long as they have the passion and willingness to try.

Words like *duty* and *responsibility* don't carry much meaning anymore, because they are synonymous with all the tasks we don't really want to do ("Guard the wall: it's your duty!" "Chores are your responsibility."). They're the words we use when we talk about the jobs that make our hearts sink. Doing dishes, washing the laundry, folding the laundry, walking the dog, going to work, running errands on your day off...the list goes on and on, and if you're living life like the rest of us, you still get those things done (eventually). Maybe you treat writing the same way: you tell yourself, "I have so much to do today! I'll write if and when I have the time to write," and that's understandable! But if words filled with artistic thought and beautiful creativity fill your head, if ink flows through your veins in *any* quantity, then it's your duty to write, because frankly, the world doesn't have enough writers, and it has even fewer poets.

Don't let the word *duty* scare you, either! Remember: you are a poet! Nothing is beyond your scope! Just think about how much uglier life would be without poetry and those who write it. Think of all the songs and catchy rhymes that helped you learn different things growing up—all those nursery rhymes are now gone, and with them, your memory of the alphabet, numbers, presidents, states, continents, worlds, and solar systems. Without poets, we wouldn't have any excuse to splash in puddles, jump over candlesticks, tumble down hills, or dance in the rain. Poetry is abundant in every holiday, religion, and landmark event throughout human history, so without people like you to write, where would we be? Putting words like *duty* together with *poetry* isn't a bad thing. Get creative! Do what you do best, and put a new and positive spin on it!

The words you write matter for plenty of reasons, but ultimately, they matter most because you are a poet. You are a poet who has a voice that is 100 percent unique to you and you alone; you are a poet who is defined by the words you write and the meanings they carry both in and between the lines; you are a poet and, by default, a historian who is uniquely gifted with the ability to translate the observations of your life and time in history into words and ideas that others can understand, and relate to.

Some poets are naturally talented, while others train for years to get where they are, but at the end of the day, if you want to write, you should write; and if you aren't writing, what's stopping you? Even if you're not writing anything you believe to be particularly skillful or life-changing, the fact that you are able to write and do so—putting your thoughts into a form that can be preserved for lifetimes after your last breath—means that those words do, in fact, matter. Now, go write more!

CHAPTER 7
Editing and Revision: How the Editing Process Can Make You a Better Poet

Finally! You've put in some long hours and late nights, you are in a full-fledged poetry relationship, and your eyes—now bloodshot from staring at a glowing screen for the last week straight—are ready to fall out of your head, but hey, you can take pride in knowing that you've written an entire poetry collection that is ready for publication! Or is it? Sure, the last thing you probably want to do after all of that work is to go back and read through everything you wrote, but believe it or not, doing so will improve your chances of being taken seriously as a poet.

CREATING "MARKERS"
As you approach writing breaks, try this: squeeze a fresh lemon slice into an empty glass near your writing area, and then continue working for five to ten minutes. Clear the lemon when you leave, and when you come back, squeeze in another. This practice in aromatherapy acts as a sort of memory marker and should help your brain pick up right where you left off!

Let's take a minute to break down exactly what you should be looking for as you edit your own work. Bear in mind that everyone's editing process is a little different, but this chapter will give you a solid place to begin.

ISN'T THAT WHAT SPELL-CHECK IS FOR?

Maybe you haven't written a book, but the complicated poem you just finished in iambic pentameter flows beautifully, rhymes masterfully, and touches on truths no one has ever put into such understandable terms. If only you hadn't posted it to your *Instagram* feed before realizing that, instead of *newspaper*, you wrote *newspapper* with three "p"s.

Where was autocorrect for that one? As our culture shifts more and more toward the online, paperless world, this handy little function *can* make communication much easier and faster for everyone who doesn't happen to have a dictionary handy, but it has also become the downfall of many contemporary poets. How many times have you skipped a true editing session, opting instead to hurry the posting of your latest poem? Then, three days and several comments later, you go back to find that instead of "happen," your autocorrect assumed you were trying to type "hasten." Three days! Three days your poem has been out for the world to see, and it makes no sense, because you didn't take the time to do a thorough edit. If only you could have caught those simple mistakes before representing yourself as a haphazard poet!

Sound familiar at all? Many writers, in their quests for notoriety, get caught up in the rat race side of things, forgetting to take their time focusing on the quality of their content instead of the quantity of it. It's a simple mistake everyone makes at some point, but even those small errors can add up to big consequences. Misspelled words, incorrectly used punctuation, synonyms that have been plugged in where they don't belong: these are all on the list of frequent faux pas, and they can all be avoided by taking some time after the writing has ended to proofread your work.

SCHEDULING YOUR POSTS

Scheduling posts—as opposed to publishing immediately—is an excellent way of putting on the brakes. You still get the high from hitting that "post" button, but scheduling it for later publishing forces you to take a much-needed pause to check for errors before the work goes public.

"But won't the reader still get what I mean, even if there is a mistake or two? And I want to get published someday! Won't the publishers have hired editors to check for errors? I want to be a writer—not an editor." Good questions! And hopefully someday you *will* be the published poet you've always dreamt of becoming. But it's important to focus on the small things—the "baby steps" that will get you there, and will still be necessary as a published poet. Building up your vocabulary, polishing your grammatical proficiency, and painting beautiful imagery with your words, meter, and attention to detail are invaluable skills that will help you to push your writing to the next level. As obvious as something might be to you, others might not know what you mean or understand where you are coming from. Looking back at your work with an editorial eye will help you find parts where the reader could be confused or interpret your words in a different way than you intended. As you know, poetry is a very subjective art form: the message you are communicating isn't necessarily the message that someone else will end up receiving. That's absolutely part of the beauty of poetry, but if you're trying to win contests or get one of your poems into a hard-bound poetry collection, the best way to do that is to get your message—the *same* message—across to as many people as possible, and the only way you're going to know how to make that happen is by taking those baby steps all the way through to the end.

EDITING CONNECTS US TO REALITY AND READERS

> I swim through worlds of blue and green,
> Fly through clouds of silver gleam,
> And leap from heights I've never seen,
> Except it's all in my head.

You chose all the words to write and carefully crafted the imagery they depict, so you already know exactly what to expect from your work, right? You have so much confidence in your poetic ability, in fact, that you can quote the entire piece from memory. Unfortunately, sometimes our brains work a little faster than our hands and eyes. Words get mashed together, entire sentences go missing, and your thoughts on current political events somehow turn into a detailing of your feelings toward the girl next door. These mistakes happen to the best of us, because we spend so much time wrestling with ideas in our heads, and it's all our pens and keyboards can do to keep up.

It's not a bad thing, but that's why editing is so important: it slows us down and pulls us out of la-la land and back into the real world where our words are being read—not experienced. Reading through your own work effectively puts you into the shoes of your audience, so that you can experience the writing from their perspective. In addition to the grammatical errors, you'll see the places where focus and flow may be lost, and how the overarching message you're trying to communicate may be unclear or missing. Finding any of this in your writing? Good thing you read through your work again before you posted it!

That role reversal should also be critically important to you as a poet, because if you can't put yourself into someone else's shoes, then you're probably going to have a very hard time writing poetry that elicits feelings in others. Even if you become well known for exclusively writing reflective poetry, your success as a poet will eventually plateau if you cannot engage your readers' thoughts and feelings. So if editing is something you truly dread after you've finished "the hard part," then try to think of it as practice in reading as a critic.

"THE HARD PART"

Speaking of "the hard part," it can be easy to wave off editing as the "easy part" that you can rush through just before posting your work. However, editing is just as involved because it's where feelings come into the mix. No one is going to fault you for feeling emotional when you write, because at the core of poetry is a very real, very powerful emotional drive, but when it comes time to hand your work over for public critique, it's easy to become a completely different kind of emotional: defensive.

Maybe it's due to the digital culture of competition, maybe it's the artistic nature of poetry, or maybe it has more to do with a sense of pride and accomplishment in completing a piece of writing. Somehow, though, whenever a writer's work is opened up to public judgment, it is natural to become overly sensitive when the feedback received is anything but positive. Social networks are notorious for this sort of hypersensitivity, too. Have you ever read a poem on *Instagram* where the very first word was misspelled, but when you commented with the correct spelling to help that poet, you just got blocked? Poets can be a touchy bunch, but the fact of the matter is that editing your own work can save you from a lot of upset.

WHAT ARE FRIENDS FOR, AFTER ALL?
If critiques from the online world are getting too difficult to bear, find a couple of close friends or family members—people whom you trust to be honest without judgment—and ask them if they'd be willing to read through your writing before you submit it to the general public.

This doesn't mean you'll never receive negative feedback, but when you are routinely editing your own writing, you become accustomed to better dealing with the mistakes you make. Over time, you should even begin to identify patterns in your writing, so that in the future, you'll "feel" the mistakes coming before they have a chance to make it onto paper. Thousands of mistakes later and years down the road, comments like, "I don't understand what you mean by this," become much easier to deal with, and simple observations of spelling and grammatical errors become comments you are thankful for instead of comments you dread. In this regard, editing is much like drinking coffee (often an acquired taste): at first it may taste downright awful, but as you continue to expose yourself to it, you develop more of a taste—or at least tolerance—for it.

HOW DO I EDIT?

Okay, now that we've been over a couple of the reasons why editing is beneficial to you as a poet, let's talk a little more about the editing process. Since every poet is unique, every poet's method for editing will be different, but there are definitely a few things to keep in the back of your mind to help you refine your work. Use these tips as a jumping-off point, but also understand that you should personalize and build upon them to fit your writing style. By doing so, your writing will maintain and radiate that sense of true intimacy and originality that can be lost when following a prescribed set of guidelines.

STEPPING STONES TO BETTER EDITING

The first rule—and this should come as no surprise—is to take your time. Be slow in writing, and slower in your corrections. Don't rush *any* part of the process. You know how long poems can take to write; between juggling complicated notions of emotion and imagery, and trying to find the right words to communicate those concepts, writing a good poem is rarely as simple as sitting down at your computer and plugging away for five minutes. Most poets make their first mistakes here. Rushing the writing process can be just as deadly to your success as opting out of the editing process altogether. Poets who write slowly and methodically, thinking over every single letter and word before it gets to the page, usually avoid making more mistakes in the initial draft, which makes the editing process a lot easier.

The second mistake is made when poets sit down to edit their work the instant the writing has ended. The root word of *Instagram* is "instant," true enough, but do you remember when we mentioned how easy it is for poets to get stuck in their heads? If you go into the editing process while you're still on the flight back from la-la land, how can you expect yourself to be objective enough to see your mistakes? Try to think of your poetry as a bottle of fine wine: once it's been opened up, it needs a chance to breathe a little before the true flavors can shine through. In other words, take at least a twenty-four-hour break from any given piece of writing before you begin editing it. Don't write more on the same piece—don't even write a completely separate poem. Instead, focus on another task entirely. Go out and ride your bike for a while, or prepare a snack, or watch a TV show; one way or another, make a clean break from writing altogether. This way, when you return to edit, you'll be coming at the poem with a fresh mind, clear focus, and an objective point of view—the three things that best facilitate quality editing. Don't be afraid to take breaks during the editing process as well! Breaks in editing will allow you to keep a fresh focus while you work.

Once you begin making revisions to your work, remember to track your changes. For old-school pen-and-paper poets, making changes isn't nearly as dangerous, but for those of you committing wholeheartedly to our shiny-screened culture, not tracking those changes is no-no number three. Poets are just as prone to getting lost in their writing during the initial drafts as they are during the editing phase. For example, while editing one of your works, you decide that within the first stanza you'd rather line three end with "broken" instead of "shattered," which changes the rhyme scheme. You continue through the piece, making necessary amendments here and there, only to find by the fourth stanza that "broken" doesn't illustrate the pieces of your glasslike heart as poignantly as "shattered" did. The problem is, because you weren't tracking your changes, all of the original content and rhyming is lost.

FIRST DRAFT, SECOND DRAFT, THIRD DRAFT...
While editing, instead of trying to catch every mistake in one reading, read the piece multiple times with a specific focus in mind during each read-through. For example, in the first reading, focus on spelling errors. In the next reading, focus on punctuation, and then in the following reading focus on concepts and imagery.

Most word processors have a function that lets you make text changes without deleting the original content, allowing you to read both the original and altered content. Become familiar with this function, because it will save you both headaches and tears in the future, especially where longer pieces are concerned. This tool also affords you ample time to take those much-needed breaks to clear your head. It will keep track of all the changes you've made to a certain point, so when you have finally slept or eaten or showered (maybe for the first time in a while), you can go back to the editing process and pick up right where you left off.

THE WORLD IS PLENTY BIG ENOUGH
If you find yourself pulled more and more toward editing as your passion, don't be afraid to shift your focus. Remember, editors can be writers, too, and the world needs both!

The journey has been long, and your brain is positively overflowing with all the information you've gleaned from the pages of this poetry guide. Now what? What could possibly be left? This is where your creativity really gets to shine, because in Part 3 you will get to put everything you've learned into action with a plethora of prompts and challenges hand-crafted to set your fingers flying. Buckle up!

PART 3

Prompts and Activities

You've found your voice, your poetic toolbox is fully stocked, and you understand the importance of editing: it's time to put it all into practice! In the following chapters you'll find a variety of prompts and poetry forms to inspire you and keep your poetic juices flowing. For those of you who are struggling to write, we've also included a chapter on writer's block, complete with activities to help you find your creativity again.

Whether your poetry is organic—a living and breathing thing that blooms when it is ready—or an intellectual exercise that is created through grit and pencil lead, daily practice will help you become a better poet. So bookmark this part and return to pick a new prompt or activity when you need some inspiration. We have also included spaces within prompts so that you can start writing as soon as your imagination strikes.

You, dear poet, are ready! Find a pen, turn the page, and let the writing begin.

CHAPTER 8
Writing Prompts

You may ask, "What is a writing prompt?" A *writing prompt* is simply a word, idea, image, or statement designed to prompt you to write. We like to think of it as poetry fuel: the spark of creativity is already inside you, and these prompts are the kindling that can help to set your poetry alight. From single word and micropoetry prompts to thematic and image prompts, there is an exercise to fit every mood!

THE FIVE PROMPT STYLES

The prompts in this chapter are divided into five distinct styles. Some styles and prompts will speak to you instantly, and the words will pour out of you and onto the page. Other prompts will have you chewing on the end of your pen as you search for that perfect opening line. We encourage you to work through the prompts that don't come easily or naturally. These more challenging exercises will push you to find new ways of writing, and you may just discover elements of your creativity that you never knew you possessed. It is often in the works that take the most "work" that we find new and meaningful ways of expressing our inner poet. The five prompt styles in this chapter are explained here:

1. **Single-Word Prompts:** A unique word is presented along with its meaning. Your challenge is to write a poem that speaks to the meaning of the word.
2. **Word Jumble Prompts:** A set of words is presented, and all of them must be used in your poem. To challenge yourself even further, each prompt also has a bonus activity that you can choose to include in your poem.
3. **Image Prompts:** A picture is presented to inspire your words. Take your time to absorb the image. Look deeply into the picture and search for the hidden meanings and emotions that it may evoke within you. An image prompt is a great opportunity to "subvert the ordinary" and avoid clichés by writing about something most people would not think of when they see the specific image.
4. **Micropoetry Prompts:** A theme or idea is presented, and word, line, or syllable limits are set. The length restrictions of these prompts forces you to think carefully about word choice and structure in order to confer meaning and evoke emotion in a very short work.
5. **Thematic Prompts:** A theme or idea is presented for you to write about. The rule book is normally very simple for these types of prompts: all you need to do is let the prompt inspire your writing. Responses to these prompts are normally long form, and often free verse.

Each of these prompt styles also has an after-the-book activity, so you can continue to use the style once you have completed the prompts in this book. At the end of this book you will find an appendix with websites and journals that you can visit for even more inspiration and guidance.

Now that you know how the prompts work, it's time to practice. You can use the lines provided underneath a prompt, as well as a separate piece of paper. We have also provided additional space at the back of the book if your poetry cup runneth over! If you are inspired to share your poems based on any of these prompts online, add the hashtag #youpoetpoetrybook to your posts so that we can read and share your poetry. So grab a pen or pencil, and get ready to write!

Single-Word Prompts

Use the following words as inspiration. Your poem should capture the meaning or "feel" of the word—without using it—through the use of clear and vivid imagery.

MERAKI: TO DO SOMETHING WITH SOUL, CREATIVITY, OR LOVE; TO PUT SOMETHING OF YOURSELF INTO YOUR WORK.

_____

_____

_____

_____

_____

_____

_____

_____

_____

_____

_____

_____

_____

_____

_____

_____

_____

_____

_____

_____

_____

CERULEAN: A DEEP BLUE, RESEMBLING THE COLOR OF THE SKY.

_____

_____

_____

_____

_____

_____

_____

_____

_____

_____

_____

_____

_____

_____

_____

_____

_____

_____

_____

_____

_____

_____

_____

ORENDA: A MYSTICAL FORCE PRESENT IN ALL PEOPLE THAT EMPOWERS THEM TO AFFECT THE WORLD OR TO EFFECT CHANGES IN THEIR OWN LIVES.

_____

_____

_____

_____

_____

_____

_____

_____

_____

_____

_____

_____

_____

_____

_____

_____

_____

_____

_____

_____

_____

_____

_____

_____

_____

DISENTHRALL: TO FREE SOMEONE FROM SLAVERY.

_____

_____

_____

_____

_____

_____

_____

_____

_____

_____

_____

_____

_____

_____

_____

_____

_____

_____

_____

_____

_____

_____

_____

MESMERISM: A COMPELLING ATTRACTION;
FASCINATION.

_____

_____

_____

_____

_____

_____

_____

_____

_____

_____

_____

_____

_____

_____

_____

_____

_____

_____

_____

_____

_____

ENNUI: A FEELING OF UTTER WEARINESS AND DISCONTENT RESULTING FROM SATIETY OR LACK OF INTEREST; BOREDOM.

_____

_____

_____

_____

_____

_____

_____

_____

_____

_____

_____

_____

_____

_____

_____

_____

_____

_____

_____

_____

PHOSPHENES: THE COLORS OR "STARS" THAT YOU SEE WHEN YOU RUB YOUR EYES.

_____

_____

_____

_____

_____

_____

_____

_____

_____

_____

_____

_____

_____

_____

_____

_____

_____

_____

_____

_____

_____

_____

VIVACIOUS: HAPPY AND LIVELY IN A WAY THAT IS ATTRACTIVE.

_____

_____

_____

_____

_____

_____

_____

_____

_____

_____

_____

_____

_____

_____

_____

_____

_____

_____

_____

_____

_____

MIZPAH: THE DEEP EMOTIONAL BOND BETWEEN PEOPLE, ESPECIALLY THOSE SEPARATED BY DISTANCE OR DEATH.

_____

_____

_____

_____

_____

_____

_____

_____

_____

_____

_____

_____

_____

_____

_____

_____

_____

_____

_____

_____

_____

EURYTHMIC: IN HARMONIOUS PROPORTION.

LETHOLOGICA: WHEN YOU CAN CAN'T THINK OF THE WORD FOR SOMETHING.

LOLLYGAG: TO SPEND TIME IN AN AIMLESS OR LAZY WAY.

_____

_____

_____

_____

_____

_____

_____

_____

_____

_____

_____

_____

_____

_____

_____

_____

_____

_____

_____

_____

_____

_____

_____

BIBLIOCLASM: THE ACT OF DESTROYING, OFTEN CEREMONIOUSLY, BOOKS OR OTHER WRITTEN MATERIAL OR MEDIA.

_____

_____

_____

_____

_____

_____

_____

_____

_____

_____

_____

_____

_____

_____

_____

_____

_____

_____

_____

_____

SERENDIPITY: THE PHENOMENON OF FINDING SOMETHING GOOD WITHOUT LOOKING FOR IT.

_____

_____

_____

_____

_____

_____

_____

_____

_____

_____

_____

_____

_____

_____

_____

_____

_____

_____

_____

_____

_____

REDAMANCY: THE ACT OF LOVING IN RETURN.

_____

_____

_____

_____

_____

_____

_____

_____

_____

_____

_____

_____

_____

_____

_____

_____

_____

_____

_____

_____

_____

_____

_____

_____

AFTER-THE-BOOK ACTIVITY

Grab a dictionary and open at random. Select a word from the page, check its meaning, and use it as a prompt. If you have friends who are poets you can also trade words and the resulting poems. If your poetry buddies are based online, you can do this by tagging them in a post with a word and its meaning, and then posting your resulting poem. Your friends can then find a word and tag you, and so on. If you add the hashtag #youpoetpoetrybook to your posts, we can read them too!

Word Jumble Prompts

Using the following lines, write a poem using all of the words listed in the prompt. Follow the "bonus" directions to add a further challenge.

ATMOSPHERE, FLIGHT, FLARE, ECLIPSE, SUPERNOVA

Bonus: don't write about the theme of space or flight.

TRANCE, ELECTRIC, DANCE FLOOR, TWIST, MIRROR

Bonus: don't write about the theme of dancing or
a night on the town.

_____

_____

_____

_____

_____

_____

_____

_____

_____

_____

_____

_____

_____

_____

_____

_____

_____

_____

_____

_____

_____

AFFLICTED, SHIVER, PIERCE, TEETH, HALLOWED

Bonus: give your poem a comedic twist!

_____

_____

_____

_____

_____

_____

_____

_____

_____

_____

_____

_____

_____

_____

_____

_____

_____

_____

_____

_____

_____

APRON, BOWL, BAKE, BROWN, APPLE

Bonus: don't write about baking or cooking.

_____

_____

_____

_____

_____

_____

_____

_____

_____

_____

_____

_____

_____

_____

_____

_____

_____

_____

_____

_____

_____

WORN, TURBULENT, FALLING, WAVE, FIELD

Bonus: write with a fantasy or mystical theme.

_____

_____

_____

_____

_____

_____

_____

_____

_____

_____

_____

_____

_____

_____

_____

_____

_____

_____

_____

_____

_____

_____

ABSTRACT, HEART, EXIT, WOUNDS, DARLING

Bonus: don't write about love.

_____

_____

_____

_____

_____

_____

_____

_____

_____

_____

_____

_____

_____

_____

_____

_____

_____

_____

_____

_____

_____

_____

_____

BARREN, WAIF, HAVEN, LUMINOUS, ASSASSIN

Bonus: give your poem an uplifting message.

_____

_____

_____

_____

_____

_____

_____

_____

_____

_____

_____

_____

_____

_____

_____

_____

_____

_____

_____

_____

_____

SWEET, SOUR, SALT, SEASON, SERVE

Bonus: don't write about cooking.

_____

_____

_____

_____

_____

_____

_____

_____

_____

_____

_____

_____

_____

_____

_____

_____

_____

_____

_____

_____

_____

_____

_____

FLASH, BANG, WHIZZ, POP, BOOM

Bonus: write a work that has a somber or serious tone.

SECRET, CHAOS, TABLET, LETTER, SCARLET

Bonus: write about modern technology.

_____

_____

_____

_____

_____

_____

_____

_____

_____

_____

_____

_____

_____

_____

_____

_____

_____

_____

_____

_____

_____

_____

_____

_____

_____

VIRUS, INFLAMED, CHILL, PAIN, INFECTION

Bonus: don't write about illness.

_____

_____

_____

_____

_____

_____

_____

_____

_____

_____

_____

_____

_____

_____

_____

_____

_____

_____

_____

_____

_____

_____

_____

HEART, INTERTWINE, WILD, DWELL, VEIL

Bonus: use these often clichéd words in a new and unexpected way.

_____

_____

_____

_____

_____

_____

_____

_____

_____

_____

_____

_____

_____

_____

_____

_____

_____

_____

_____

_____

_____

_____

DESIRE, DECAY, DANCES, DEATH, DESTINY

Bonus: create a tautogram by only using words that start with the letter "d."

FLOWER, BLOOM, WAX, WANE, STEM

Bonus: don't write about flowers or the natural world.

CHAOS, CIRCLE, GULF, FILM, SILVER

Bonus: make your poem rhyme.

_____

_____

_____

_____

_____

_____

_____

_____

_____

_____

_____

_____

_____

_____

_____

_____

_____

_____

_____

_____

_____

_____

_____

AFTER-THE-BOOK ACTIVITY

Grab your favorite book or magazine and select five words at random to include in a poem.

Image Prompts

On the lines provided, write a poem inspired by each of the following images.

_____

_____

_____

_____

_____

_____

_____

_____

_____

_____

_____

_____

_____

_____

_____

_____

_____

_____

_____

_____

_____

_____

_____

_____

PART 3: PROMPTS AND ACTIVITIES

_____

_____

_____

_____

_____

_____

_____

_____

_____

_____

_____

_____

_____

_____

_____

_____

_____

_____

_____

_____

_____

_____

_____

_____

_____

_____

_____

_____

_____

_____

_____

_____

_____

_____

_____

_____

_____

_____

_____

_____

_____

_____

_____

_____

_____

_____

PART 3: PROMPTS AND ACTIVITIES

_____

_____

_____

_____

_____

_____

_____

_____

_____

_____

_____

_____

_____

_____

_____

_____

_____

_____

_____

_____

_____

_____

_____

_____

_____

_____

_____

_____

_____

_____

_____

_____

_____

PART 3: PROMPTS AND ACTIVITIES

_____

_____

_____

_____

_____

_____

_____

_____

_____

_____

PART 3: PROMPTS AND ACTIVITIES

_____

_____

_____

_____

_____

_____

_____

_____

_____

_____

_____

_____

_____

_____

_____

_____

_____

_____

_____

_____

_____

_____

_____

_____

_____

_____

_____

_____

_____

_____

_____

_____

_____

_____

PART 3: PROMPTS AND ACTIVITIES

_____

_____

_____

_____

_____

_____

_____

_____

_____

_____

_____

_____

_____

_____

_____

_____

_____

_____

_____

_____

_____

_____

_____

_____

_____

_____

_____

_____

_____

_____

_____

_____

_____

_____

_____

_____

_____

_____

_____

_____

_____

_____

_____

_____

_____

AFTER-THE-BOOK ACTIVITY

Head to Unsplash.com and click on "New." Pick an image at random to write about. The great thing about this site is that if you write something you want to share, the image is free for use without attribution, so it can be posted to your social media sites.

Micropoetry Prompts

On the following lines, write a poem using the instructions in each prompt.

A six-word story for a kiss.

_____

_____

_____

_____

Four lines for an ex.

_____

_____

_____

_____

Eleven words for a lost friend.

_____

_____

_____

_____

Gone in sixty letters.

_____

_____

_____

_____

Fourteen syllables of healing and hope.

_____

_____

_____

_____

Five lines for unity.

_____

_____

_____

_____

Sixteen syllables to lead someone astray.

_____

_____

_____

_____

Seven words for your heaven.

_____

_____

_____

_____

Make the reader tremble in three lines.

_____

_____

_____

_____

Fifty letters for a new beginning.

_____

_____

_____

_____

Nine words you should have said before the train doors
slid shut.

_____

_____

_____

_____

Fifteen syllables to decipher me.

_____

_____

_____

_____

Change someone's mind in seven lines.

_____

_____

_____

_____

An eight-word love letter.

_____

_____

_____

_____

Thirteen words for a teenager.

_____

_____

_____

_____

Twenty-three syllables for a final day.

_____

_____

_____

_____

Four lines to steal a heart.

_____

_____

_____

_____

Seven words to make an escape.

_____

_____

_____

_____

Move the heart with a six-word story.

_____

_____

_____

_____

A single line to make her mine.

_____

_____

_____

_____

Thirty words for a natural phenomenon.

_____

_____

_____

_____

Nine lines for a keepsake.

_____

_____

_____

_____

Describe a stranger in fifteen words.

_____

_____

_____

_____

"One of those days" in seven words.

_____

_____

_____

_____

Seventeen syllables to describe the creature that lurks
under your bed.

_____

_____

_____

_____

Swim in the abyss in three lines.

_____

_____

_____

_____

AFTER-THE-BOOK ACTIVITY

Grab ten pieces of white paper, three pieces of blue paper, and twenty pieces of yellow paper and write the following:

- **White:** The numbers one to ten.
- **Blue:** "Words," "lines," and "syllables."
- **Yellow:** Twenty different themes or topics that appeal to you (if you get stuck then you can use words from book titles or your favorite songs).

Once you have your cards written, select one white, one blue, and one yellow piece of paper. Use the descriptors on your cards to inspire a micropoem. Repeat whenever you please!

Thematic Prompts

On the following lines, write a poem inspired by the theme
in each prompt.

I WILL RAISE MY VOICE FOR...

Poetry can be a powerful medium for the expression of deeply held beliefs and opinions. This prompt is a challenge to you to connect with your core values and beliefs, and to write a work that explores what you would raise your voice for.

ONCE UPON A TIME

Write a poem using the phrase "Once upon a time." The twist: don't use it at the start of your poem.

SOMEBODY TOLD ME

Write a poem that starts with the clichéd line "Somebody told me." However, the poem must be one that isn't clichéd and surprises the reader.

_____

_____

_____

_____

_____

_____

_____

_____

_____

_____

_____

_____

_____

_____

_____

_____

_____

_____

_____

_____

_____

_____

SING-ALONG

Write a poem that contains the title of one of your favorite songs. It can be included anywhere in the poem. As an additional element, try to write a poem that has a different or opposing theme to that of the song.

_____

_____

_____

_____

_____

_____

_____

_____

_____

_____

_____

_____

_____

_____

_____

_____

_____

_____

_____

_____

MOMENT BY MOMENT

Find a photo that speaks to your soul, and use the theme "moment by moment" to inspire your words. This is a play on a concrete-image poem.

_____

_____

_____

_____

_____

_____

_____

_____

_____

_____

_____

_____

_____

_____

_____

_____

_____

_____

_____

_____

_____

_____

_____

MY FIRST LOVE

Write about your first love. This may not be a person, so feel free to explore the topic in whatever way you may interpret it.

_____

_____

_____

_____

_____

_____

_____

_____

_____

_____

_____

_____

_____

_____

_____

_____

_____

_____

_____

_____

_____

_____

_____

_____

_____

_____

_____

_____

_____

_____

_____

_____

_____

_____

_____

_____

_____

_____

_____

_____

_____

_____

_____

_____

_____

_____

FLAWED BEAUTY

Create a poem that captures an unusual and imperfect beauty to help your reader see something in a new and positive way.

_____

_____

_____

_____

_____

_____

_____

_____

_____

_____

_____

_____

_____

_____

_____

_____

_____

_____

THE ANIMAL IN ME SIMILE

Use an animal, or animal behavior, as a simile in your poem.

_____

_____

_____

_____

_____

_____

_____

_____

_____

_____

_____

_____

_____

_____

_____

_____

_____

_____

_____

_____

OUTCAST

Can you tap into the feeling of exclusion? Or, on the reverse side, can you bring hope and inclusion? Think like an outcast and write a poem on this theme.

_____

_____

_____

_____

_____

_____

_____

_____

_____

_____

_____

_____

_____

_____

_____

_____

_____

_____

_____

SLAY THE BEAST

What are your demons? What beast do you hide within?
Write a poem that slays the beast.

_____

_____

_____

_____

_____

_____

_____

_____

_____

_____

_____

_____

_____

_____

_____

_____

_____

_____

_____

_____

_____

_____

AT THE BREAK OF DAY

A new day can bring new hope and new possibilities. Write a poem that captures this theme and uses "at the break of day" in the final line of the poem.

_____

_____

_____

_____

_____

_____

_____

_____

_____

_____

_____

_____

_____

_____

_____

_____

_____

_____

_____

_____

AFTER-THE-BOOK ACTIVITY

Head to your computer and search for the words "poetry prompts" or "creative writing prompts." The world of poetry prompts is wide open to you! If you decide to share your poetry online, please add the hashtag #youpoetpoetrybook so that we can read them too!

CHAPTER 9
Poetry Forms

Welcome to the world of form! In this chapter we will challenge your creativity by exploring different traditional and contemporary poetry forms, so that you can flex your poetry prowess by writing to the rule book. We've also included examples so you can see what poems within a certain form look like.

THE RULES OF FORM

Now, we can hear what you are thinking: "Rules, schmooles, I'm a contemporary poet! I will not be contained." But hold on—there are several great reasons for writing to the rules, and we encourage you to consider them before you declare that you are skipping this chapter in an act of poetic rebellion.

1. **The rules give you freedom.** Many of us get stuck in the safe and familiar. How often have you written a love poem, or a poem about the ocean? Writing to the rules will shake up your perspective and set you free from your existing habits.
2. **The rules require you to improve your understanding and use of poetic devices.** Structured forms often have devices like rhyme and meter. These devices can help you create more effective imagery, greater flow, and more impact in your piece.
3. **The rules will help you expand your lexicon.** Have you ever tried to rhyme with the word *purple*? Often when you

are writing to the rules, you will need to find new words to help you express your ideas. The greater your vocabulary and understanding of a word's meaning, the greater the depth of your writing. (By the way, *hirple* rhymes with *purple*, and means "to limp or walk awkwardly.")

We have even included a section dedicated specifically to digital poetry forms. These are forms that have been cultivated by the spread of social media, and have been crafted as a result of the digital boundaries and "rules" that these platforms create. So if you really want to be a rebel, these are the forms that are shaping the contemporary poetry revolution.

TRADITIONAL FORMS

The traditional forms in this chapter are a sample of some of the hundreds of types of poetry that have been used and developed over the last two centuries. Take a look and give them a try!

COLLABORATIVE

A collaborative poem is a poem constructed by two or more people. The poem can take any traditional poetic form. There are several types of collaborative poetry, but the most popular are the following:

- **Chain:** Poets write a single line that is then sent on to another poet who writes another single line, and so on.
- **Reflective:** Poets choose a topic and write about it from opposing perspectives, resulting in at least two stanzas. An example of this form is writing from a feminine perspective, and then from a masculine perspective.

- **Tapestry:** Poets write their own version of a poem on a given topic and then attempt to weave the poem into one cohesive work. Normally the poem will have a total of nine lines.
- **Switch:** A poem switches authorship at a certain line, word, or stanza.

A collaborative poem can have any number of stanzas, and rhyming is optional. The theme is at the poets' discretion. However, the goal of any collaborative poem is to make the work read as a single cohesive piece of writing, and for the two (or more) voices to ultimately create synergy, resulting in a stronger piece of writing than if it had been written by a single author. To practice, find a poetry buddy, choose a style and topic, and write!

ETHEREE

An etheree is a traditional poetry form that consists of ten lines of one, two, three, four, five, six, seven, eight, nine, and finally ten syllables. An etheree can also be reversed and written as ten, nine, eight, seven, six, five, four, three, two, then one syllable. There is a wide scope for creativity here, as you can write more than one verse, and invert your syllable count from one to the next, resulting in a double etheree—one, two, three, four, five, six, seven, eight, nine, ten, ten, nine, eight, seven, six, five, four, three, two, one—through to a triple etheree, quadruple etheree, and so on. The topic is at the discretion of the poet, and rhyming is optional, so all you really have to do to give it a try is make sure your syllables are on count. This is also a great opportunity to crack open a thesaurus for different word options that fit your syllabic needs. Here is an example:

Come, (one syllable)
to me (two syllables)
my dear love. (three syllables)
Drink of my lips (four syllables)
to water your well. (five syllables)
Take of my daily bread (six syllables)
my basket offered freely, (seven syllables)
nourishing no other but you. (eight syllables)
How will I love you? You ask of me. (nine syllables)
With my heart, my all, my everything. (ten syllables)

LANTURNE

The lanturne (also known as the *lanterne* and *lantern*) is a five-line poem originating from Japan. It has the syllable pattern one, two, three, four, one. Once the poem is written, the words are centered on the line to create the shape of a Japanese lantern, hence the name. Since the number of syllables is an important aspect of this poem, this is a great form to try when you are looking for a challenge or want to keep things short and sweet. Here is an example:

Dawn (one syllable)
draws near (two syllables)
eyes open (three syllables)
to the days' light (four syllables)
Hope (one syllable)

LIMERICK

A limerick is a five-line poem that follows a rhyme scheme of AABBA (this means that the first, second, and fifth lines rhyme with one another, and the third and fourth lines rhyme with one another). Very often, the third and fourth lines of a limerick are shorter than the others and they're commonly written in anapestic meter (a metrical foot consisting of two unaccented syllables and one accented syllable), but as with all things artistic, these are details that are wide open to interpretation. On top of that, limericks are almost always either funny or crude (often both). The next time you find yourself in a ridiculous situation or hear a funny joke, trying writing a limerick about it. We've provided an example:

Once I found fish in the sky (A)
who bubbled as they floated by, (A)
but the second I blinked (B)
they swam down the sink (B)
with garbage disposal on high. (A)

NAANI

Naani, a traditional Telugu poetry form, means "an expression of one and all." It was popularized by respected Indian poet Dr. N. Gopi. The naani consists of four lines made up of twenty to twenty-five syllables. A naani doesn't have any rigid subject or thematic boundaries, but it normally depicts human relationships or current events, so try writing your own naani when you are feeling overwhelmed by bad news, or you are struggling with a close personal relationship. Here is an example:

> Loud voices silence the needy (eight syllables)
> with condemnation in comb-overs and emails. (twelve syllables)
> The world waits, (three syllables)
> breath held. (two syllables)

NONET

A nonet is a traditional poetry form consisting of nine lines. The first line is nine syllables long. The following lines each decrease by one syllable until the final, ninth line, which is one syllable. Nonets can be on any subject, and rhyming is optional. Here is an example:

> He wades into the rhythm of life (nine syllables)
> a sailor leaving childhood's shores (eight syllables)
> for a siren's silver call. (seven syllables)
> Floating on melodies (six syllables)
> cresting, anchor cast (five syllables)
> into the depths (four syllables)
> of her salt (three syllables)
> covered (two syllables)
> skin. (one syllable)

RONDELET

A rondelet is a short French poetry form with a strict structure and rhyming pattern. It consists of one stanza of seven lines, known as a single septet. The lines consist of two rhymes and one refrain in the pattern: AbAabbA. The capital letters (A) are the refrain (a repeated line); the lowercase (a) line rhymes with the uppercase (A) lines; and the lowercase (b) lines rhyme with each other. The refrain has four syllables ("tetra syllabic," or "dimeter") and the other lines are twice as long, with eight syllables ("octasyllabic," or "tetrameter"). The structure of this form is:

Line one: four syllables (A)
Line two: eight syllables (b)
Line three: repeat line one (A)
Line four: eight syllables—rhymes with line one (a)
Line five: eight syllables—rhymes with line two (b)
Line six: eight syllables—rhymes with lines two and five (b)
Line seven: repeat line one (A)

A bit confused? Check out our example:

Why do you call? (A; four syllables)
When you know you do not want me. (b; eight syllables)
Why do you call? (A; four syllables)
You've already taken it all. (a; eight syllables)
I ask of you, just let me be (b; eight syllables)
unhand my heart, and set me free. (b; eight syllables)
Why do you call? (A; four syllables)

TRIOLET

A triolet consists of one stanza that is eight lines long. It has the rhyme scheme ABaAabAB, in which the first, fourth, and seventh lines are the same, and the second and eighth lines are the same. A repeated line reinforces the main theme of a poem, and can also be used to establish a rhythmic pattern that creates natural ebbs and flows. Here is an example:

Take me back to those yesterdays. (A)
When love and life and I was new (B)
and full of easy, girl-child ways. (a)
Take me back to those yesterdays (A)
before carefree lost to lean-hipped sway (a)
before I gave me, stained-red to you. (b)
Take me back to those yesterdays, (A)
when love and life and I was new. (B)

A NOTE ON JAPANESE FORMS

You cannot write about traditional poetry forms without including the well-known haiku and related Japanese forms. Not only have these forms existed for hundreds of years, but they have an enduring popularity among poets today. These elegant and subtle forms teach you about the importance of construction, word choice, and word efficiency when creating evocative and moving poetry. Guides for these forms could, and do, fill entire books and websites, so what we will share is not exhaustive. Instead, we will give you a brief overview to get you started.

HAIKU

The haiku is the most well-known and popular form of Japanese poetry. Originally these were referred to as *hokku*, and formed the opening stanza of other forms. Over time they became stand-alone poems. Traditionally, the form was restricted to an objective description of nature that evoked an emotional response. It also contained a reference to one of the seasons. Contemporary haiku, while not restricted thematically, do adhere to certain criteria: three lines in length, with the syllable format: five, seven, five. Haiku should create meaning through comparison by using a phrase or fragment on each line. Here is an example:

When I left *Facebook* (five syllables)
No one noticed I had gone. (seven syllables)
Do I still exist? (five syllables)

TANKA AND WAKA

Originally, *waka* referred to any poem written in Japanese. *Tanka*, meaning "short poem," falls under the category of *waka*. Over time *waka* and *tanka* became synonymous with each other and are now commonly referred to as *tanka*. A tanka is a five-line poem consisting of the syllable pattern: five, seven, five, seven, seven. We've included an example:

Little wings broken (five syllables)
clipped by a man's unkind hands, (seven syllables)
and his unkind words. (five syllables)
But when she finds her feathers, (seven syllables)
her strength, his hold is broken. (seven syllables)

SEDOKA

A sedoka is an unrhymed poem composed of two katauta. A katauta is a poem that has three lines with the syllable pattern five, seven, seven, and is able to stand alone as a complete poem. Therefore, a sedoka has the syllable pattern:

five, seven, seven; five, seven, seven. In order to be correct, each katauta must be able to be read independently, but also create a cohesive singular work within the sedoka. Often a sedoka will address the same subject from different perspectives. Here is an example:

The light opens eyes (five syllables)
Spring's glory arrives at dawn, (seven syllables)
she has cloaked the South in green. (seven syllables)

To dreams we are called (five syllables)
Winter's slumber treads the North (seven syllables)
bringing his blanket of snow. (seven syllables)

CONTEMPORARY FORMS

Although contemporary poetry forms do not have the same long history as the traditional forms, they pose new outlets for creative expression, and new challenges to exercise and improve your writing skills.

ACROSTIC

An acrostic poem is where the first letter of each line spells a word. This form can also be manipulated so that the word is spelled using the last letter of each line, or the center letter of each line. The poem can be on any subject, and rhyming is optional. The example here uses the word "poetry":

Pick the story of us
Out of the bones of my chest
Eat each
Tender word
Rendering
Yesterday's love lost.

BLACKOUT AND BLURRED LINES

Blackout and blurred lines poems erase words in existing pieces of writing to create new meanings. Although they are similar, they use different methods to create the final work.

1. **Blackout:** Blackout poetry, or blackout newspaper poetry, was popularized in 2010 by author and cartoonist Austin Kleon. Many believe that this is a form of erasure poetry, which was first seen as early as 1975. In a blackout poem, the poet takes an existing piece of writing and draws over the text, or select pieces of text, to create a new work. The new work often attempts to subvert the original work and stand in its own context, free from the original piece of writing.

2. **Blurred Lines:** With the ease of access to photo editing apps, blackout poetry has further evolved into the blurred lines form. Instead of manually deleting words using a marker or pen, the poet uses a photo editing app to blur out words and create a new work. As with a blackout poem, a blurred lines poem also attempts to create an entirely new work free from the context of the original writing.

I wear wanderlust where a wedding ring should be.

It is not the **enchantm**ent of different **skin**, a new flavor
in my mouth. But new lands **under** my feet, new **stars** in
the sky, the touch of waters newly swum and the taste of
foods, eaten with gusto, for the very first time.

I do not **crave** the slick slip of another body against mine,
but rather the ring of bells from a distant church on ears,
the **warm** touch of sun and breeze on distant shores on
skin, a language that tastes foreign on the **lips** and tongue

I don't **fear** the commitment of **a life lived** in a bag born
on my shoulders, rather, that life that sees skin
wither in sunless skies **in between** cooled down sheets,
in arms that do not know the tussle of crowded bus rides
and more crowded sheets.

I wear wanderlust where a wedding ring should be.

Rayna Halloway

CONCRETE

A concrete poem involves arranging the words of the poem
into a shape to enhance or depict the key theme or meaning of
the poem. Although the term *concrete* is new, there is a long tra-
dition of shaped poems dating back to the third century B.C.E.

This form is dependent on an overlap of the written mean-
ing of the poem and its visual representation, and the visual
element is just as (if not more) important as the writing in
conveying the poem's meaning. This form can have any num-
ber of stanzas arranged in any shape, and rhyming is optional.
Here is an example:

                                        tomorrow.

                              I will wait for you

                            in our never forever?

                          you wait for me there

                        you climbed alone. Will

                      that gentle climb, that

                    end of the tunnel,

                  The light at the

ELFCHEN

An elfchen (translated as "little eleven") consists of five
lines and a total of eleven words. It is a German form of
poetry with the following structure:

First line: one word
Second line: two words
Third line: three words
Fourth line: four words
Fifth line: one word

This simple and short form is one that can teach you to
think carefully about how you will use each word to create
an image and evoke a response in your reader. They are also
addictive to write!

Here is an example:

Ink (one word)
wells up (two words)
and springs forth (three words)
staining my fingers with (four words)
poetry. (one word)

FOUND-OBJECT

Found-object poetry is a collaborative work between writer and reader. Loosely based on found-object art, a found-object poem is first written by the poet, and then left somewhere unexpected to be found by the reader. It is only when the poem is found, and a moment of connection and realization is created, that it becomes a piece of art. Found-object poems can be written in any form, and rhyming is optional. There is no set length; however, short works, such as haiku, are popular. A found-object poem usually has an uplifting and positive theme.

SPOKEN WORD

Spoken word is covered in more detail in Part 1, but just to jog your memory, it is performance poetry that involves reciting your poetry aloud, with or without music, and requires tools such as tone, intonation, and body language to create connection. Spoken word poems are written with careful attention to word flow and rhythm, and rhyming is very common. For examples, visit HerHeartPoetry.com and use the search term "spoken word."

TAUTOGRAM

A tautogram uses only words that start with the same letter. It can be on any topic, and rhyming is optional. This form is notoriously hard to write, but really provides a sense of accomplishment when finished. Here is an example:

Five fled fearful, from
fires
fighting
foul foes,
fleeing for freedom.

Five falter.
Five fade.
Five fall.
Five fracture from final farewells.

Forlorn,
frightened,
formerly forsaken,
four finally find foreign favour.
Four finally find familiarity.
Four finally find family.
Finally.

TETRACTYS

A tetractys consists of at least five lines of one, two, three, four, and ten syllables (a total of twenty syllables) and can also be reversed and written as ten, four, three, two, and one syllable. A tetractys can have more than one verse, but each subsequent verse must be an inverse of the previous one. Thus, a double tetractys would be written: one, two, three, four, ten, ten, four, three, two, one.

Here is an example:

Girl (one syllable)
blinded (two syllables)
by longing. (three syllables)
Find your freedom (four syllables)
from wanting, perfection adorns your skin. (ten syllables)

DIGITAL FORMS

Each of the following digital forms is either free verse, or uses simple rhyme schemes. Refrains (a repeated line) are not common, and meter is usually ignored. There is no set theme for any of the following digital forms; however, traditional themes such as love, loss, longing, heartbreak, and romance are popular. Themes of social justice, activism, and real-world commentary are also becoming more popular. These Contemporary forms are short because of the nature of social media. Swiping takes seconds, so a poem must be able to be read quickly to capture the reader's attention.

AXIOM

An axiom is a free verse micropoem (usually one to two lines) that is a statement of an accepted or self-evident truth. These poems tap into the emotions and experiences of readers quickly and effectively, evoking a response without relying on a set context, which makes them relatable to a wide range of readers. Here is an example:

Love lived here
until the day you left.

CONCRETE-IMAGE

A concrete-image poem is a short work that is edited over
a complementary image. In this form, the words and image are
discovered in tandem. Much like the use of a title to enhance
the overall meaning of a poem, a concrete-image poem uses an
image to evoke a specific feeling. Subforms of this genre include:
typewriter (poetry produced on paper on a typewriter and then
photographed), handwritten (poetry written by hand and then
photographed), and "in real life" (poetry printed and then pho-
tographed in the poet's hand against a real-world background).

LINE BREAK

A line break poem is a micropoem characterized by break-
ing up single lines into two or more smaller lines to create
emphasis. The popularity of the line break form is largely
attributed to Rupi Kaur. Here is an example:

The fear in my
                   soul
It swallows me, all of me,
whole.

PASTICHE

A pastiche is a poem that is written in a traditional poetry
form, but is published using modern digital techniques. This
often includes using a background image. It is likely that your
first foray into the world of social media sharing will be this

type of poem! You can use eye-catching images to engage online readership. Here is an example of this form:

> My skin is marked by
> your footsteps.
>
> Indentations left
> where your mouth
> once visited.
> Ears deafened
> by your words
> once whispered.
> Hands bound
> by your touch
> once given.
> A heart beat quiet
> by the absence
> of yours.
>
> My skin is marked by
> your footsteps.
> But now,
> my feet travel alone.

> R. Hutchison | Footsteps
> @herheartshapedbox

SWIPE

A swipe poem is separated into parts and placed on separate posts in a social media outlet such as *Instagram*. This form was created in 2017, and has become more and more popular. To read a swipe poem, the reader must *swipe* through the posts. The points where the poem is separated are critical: they can create emphasis; provide a physical journey to enhance a changing or evolving narrative; or deliver a surprise ending. Here is an example:

Swipe one:

Darling girl,
you will spend your days hearing that you are a flower.
That your existence is balanced
on the nape of a petal
and that you are just as delicate,
to be admired
and looked at
until your beauty fades
and your worth wilts.

And darling girl, I will not lie.
You are a flower.
A wild flower.
Whose face opens to the sun and sky,
with each new day
not one who is trapped inside a glass cage
only to be forgotten in between the press of pages.

Swipe two:

Little wild flower, I tell you to ramble,
ramble out beyond those borders
that would try to contain your bloom.
Burst up through the cracked pavement
that would tame you,
float upon the wind, in dandelion seed wishes,
where you will see the world.

Little wild flower,
let those who would admire you do so.
But, not for the flash of fleeting colour
that lasts for a single season.
But for the strength it has taken
For you
To grow.

Swipe three:

And little wild flower, being delicate is your choice.

TWITTERATURE

A Twitterature poem is a micropoem of 280 characters or less. The poem must be able to stand alone as a complete work within a single *Twitter* tweet. Correct spelling and grammar can be sacrificed in favor of the overall "feel" and emotion of the work. We've provided an example:

That is not the sound of thunder.
that is the sound that your leaving has left.

UTTERANCE

An utterance poem (or "snippet") is a micropoem characterized by its appearance as a snippet of conversation. The poem is taken out of its known context for effect, and often embraces modern clichés. Rather than subverting the conventional, which would be a common goal for most poets, the poet embraces clichés to create a connection. Examples would include common descriptions such as "drowning in your love," or "she has a galaxy of stars in her eyes." The purpose of the work is to encourage the reader to find his or her own meaning and experience in the work. This is one of the most popular contemporary digital poetry forms, as it very simply, and effectively, illustrates universal experiences. Here is an example:

> You can't see it,
> but my strength
> lies in my softness.

It can be very easy to rely on free verse as your poetry stock-in-trade. However, writing a poem in a specific form, particularly a traditional one, can help make you a better poet, as it will allow you to practice and perfect your construction skills, grow your vocabulary, improve your word choice and word use, and further develop your ability to evoke a response in your reader. Don't be scared to play with form, and at the very least give each one a try. We are sure that there will be at least one form that you will want to write again and again. These exercises are also a great antidote to writer's block! Learn more about this classic writing curse in the next chapter.

CHAPTER 10
What to Do about Writer's Block

What do Walt Whitman, Katherine Mansfield, and Ernest Hemingway have in common with you right now? Well, if you are reading this chapter there is a very good chance that you are suffering from the curse of writer's block…just like these literary giants once did. Being a lauded writer does not make you immune to the misery that happens when the words we rely upon, the very words that help us define our world, decide to head south (or north) for the winter. In fact, we would be hard-pressed to find a writer anywhere who hasn't had a case of writer's block at some point in his or her life.

In this chapter, we will define writer's block and discuss two distinct approaches that can help you overcome it. We will also share practical activities that you can do to help flex your writing muscles and reconnect with your creative self. Let's rediscover your muse!

WHAT IS WRITER'S BLOCK?

Writer's block is that claustrophobic feeling of not being able to get the words out. Writer's block may be seen in the glaring reflection of a white page, or a page that has just a few words haphazardly strewn about on it. Whatever it looks like for you, it is the frustration of not being able to find the next word, or the first word, or even worse—not having a single idea to start with in the first place.

The good news is that writer's block can be cured. How long it will take comes down to you and the reasons for your block in the first place, but there are two paths that you can tread to find your muse again—so keep reading!

AN ACADEMIC APPROACH

The first method for curing writer's block is the academic approach. This is very simple to understand, but can be difficult to implement. Most professional writers will tell you that they write every day. They have a set schedule for writing, including a start and end time and/or a word count target, and stick to this schedule no matter how uninspired they may feel. This approach creates a habit of writing, training the brain to write in exactly the same way that someone who gets up at five a.m. every morning to run a 10k trains their muscles. On the days where you don't feel creative or motivated, you write anyway. You may not use any of the words that you write on these days, but you are training yourself for your future poetry-writing marathons.

The easiest way to begin this approach is to start with ten minutes at a set time. You might decide to get up slightly earlier in the morning, or you might decide to switch off the TV at seven p.m. every night. The important thing is that you choose a time when you can turn off your devices, close your door, and focus on your writing. It should also be a time that can grow as your writing habit grows. Each week you should challenge yourself to add another ten minutes to your writing time. At the end of six weeks you will be in the habit of writing for one full hour every day! And after sixty-six days (the magic number for habit formation), daily writing will be just as much a part of your life as your morning cup of coffee. However, if this approach doesn't appeal to you, check out the next approach, where the muse finds you!

AN ORGANIC APPROACH

The organic approach is much less rigid than an academic approach: all it asks of you is to breathe and let go. Rather than stressing about the fact that you can't write, do things that inspire your creativity. Take a walk on the beach (or in a park, or on a mountain). Listen to music. Take some pictures and manipulate them in an app. Paint, draw, or scribble. Pick some flowers and arrange them in a vase. Dance around your living room. Meditate and practice mindfulness. Instead of demanding creativity, this more gentle approach gives your creative mind a break, and creates space for the muse to find *you*.

Now that you have an understanding of the two main approaches to curing your writer's block, let's take a look at some exercises that can help you get your pen back on paper!

POETRY WORKOUT OF THE DAY

Whether you use an academic approach or an organic approach to cure your writer's block, the following exercises can further help to fire up your imagination and creativity. These poetry workouts of the day (WODs) are a great way to exercise your writing muscles.

An important note on these WODs: we don't expect you to write the next great poem, although that might happen! The purpose of these WODs is to just *write*. Even if you aren't writing well, you are writing. As Maya Angelou once said, "What I try to do is write. I may write for two weeks 'the cat sat on the mat, that is that, not a rat.' And it might be just the most boring and awful stuff. But I try. When I'm writing, I write. And then it's as if the muse is convinced that I'm serious and says, 'Okay. Okay. I'll come.'"

EXERCISE 1: CUT AND PASTE

The purpose of this exercise is to upcycle your old writing and help you reconnect with your voice. Although this exercise can be done on a computer or tablet, we believe it is more effective when you do it with your hands on good old-fashioned paper (shocking, we know!).

Take some of your old poems (or lines that you have written but haven't used), write them on paper, and then use scissors to cut them into individual lines. Place them on a flat surface and create an entirely new work by moving lines together or apart. You can cut words out, add words in, or take a line from a final stanza and make it your opening line. The only rule is to create a new work free from the context of the poems you have cut up. Cut and paste together at least four lines. This method was famously used by Walt Whitman, who upcycled his unused material to create brilliant and enduring new works of poetry.

EXERCISE 2: MIND SPRINKLES

Mind sprinkles, as funny as they sound, are exactly that: little bits and pieces of creativity that are floating around in your mind right now. On a piece of paper, write down the first twenty words that come to mind. Don't overthink it; just let the words bubble up to the surface. Write them as quickly as you can. Now write a poem using five of your mind sprinkles. Again, don't overthink it; just write. Now start again with five of the other words.

The purpose of this exercise is to show you that at any point in time you have ideas waiting in your subconscious. This WOD allows you to quickly connect with the hidden gems that are waiting to be discovered.

EXERCISE 3: NATURAL RESOURCES

The natural world has long been a source of inspiration for poets. From the seasonal references in traditional Japanese haiku, to the garden poems of the seventeenth century, landscapes, seasons, and natural events have been featured in poems throughout history. In this exercise, you will select a natural occurrence and write at least four lines about it. You can either write about it directly or use it as a metaphor for something else.

You can find inspiration by walking outside and writing about what you see. This models an organic approach, where you allow inspiration to find you in your travels. You can also search for images of the natural world online, or write about the images that come to mind when you think about nature. To get you started, here is a list of natural objects and events:

- A pebble skipping on a lake
- Hurricane
- Waterfall
- Autumn leaves
- Camellia bud
- Winding river
- Albatross
- Pinecone
- Meadow
- Winter frost
- Dawn
- Honeybee
- Southerly wind
- Tsunami
- Moss-covered log

EXERCISE 4: THE FIVE SENSES

Can you describe an omelet using all five senses of taste, touch, sight, smell, and sound? Can you help a reader not only see the spots on a cheetah, but smell the surrounding plains as it runs, and feel the heat of the sun on its flanks? In this exercise, pick an item or situation and write a poem that incorporates all five senses. This exercise will help you improve your descriptive writing and vocabulary skills, and will also push you in new and unexpected directions. If you aren't sure what to write about, you can start with these examples:

- Train ride
- Missed call
- Ironing board
- Fireworks
- First love
- Snow
- Flowers in a vase
- Bright red shoes
- Stray dog
- Dreams
- Broken zipper
- Cupcakes
- Books

EXERCISE 5: PI AND I—A NUMERICAL WORD JUMBLE

Pie isn't just good for eating; it is also good for nourishing your inner creative! This poetry WOD relies on page and line selection to create inspiration. First, you will need a book. We grabbed *The Great Gatsby* off the shelf. Now, take the first word that you see from pages three, one, four, fifteen, and nine. Our words are: *begin*, *last*, *club*, *debts*, and *first*. Now write a poem of at least four lines that uses your five random words. Don't think too much—just let the words and theme flow. This is what we came up with:

> So it **begins**,
> this lonely hearts **club**;
> where we pay our **debts**,
> with **first** and **last** loves.

Want to write another stanza? Grab the first words you see on pages twenty-six, five, thirty-five, eighty-nine, and seven. You can look up "pi" online if you want even more numbers to use. You can also mix it up by selecting the first word from each of these pages, or selecting a single page and then using the third word, first word, fourth word, fifteenth word, and ninth word. The combinations are endless. Bored with the words in that book? Grab a new one and start from the beginning.

Now that you've cracked your writer's block and are full of inspiration, it's time to think about sharing your work with others—and learn how to do so using the different platforms and channels available.

PART
4

Sharing Your Work
with the World

You've been writing regularly and working on your craft.
You've got a collection of poems that you are proud of. Now
it is time to unleash those words on the world. This part will
explore different ways that you can share your work online,
including an entire chapter on your must-have #digitalpoetry
toolkit. This toolkit is crammed full of practical tips to help you
craft your online style and create an attractive and engaging
digital profile. We have also included a list of apps, websites,
and submission platforms that you can use to create and sub-
mit your poetry. You'll find everything you need to not only
share your voice with the world, but also ensure that it is
heard.

CHAPTER 11
Traditional Publishing Avenues

For many poets, the desire to see our words in print is a driving force in honing our craft. The ultimate goal is not only inclusion in an online magazine or social media platform, but also words in ink on a page. This might be in an anthology, a chapbook, or a bona fide "I-did-it-Mom" poetry book, either self-published or published by an established printing house.

However, seeing your poetry and name in print will take time and commitment. You will receive rejections and critiques, like every writer out there has at one point. But you will also grow from these experiences.

WRITING A SUCCESSFUL SUBMISSION

To help make the publishing process a little less daunting, we've outlined the steps you need to take to write a successful submission. These steps can be applied to poetry competitions, submissions to publishing houses, and successful self-publications:

HAVE AN AUTHENTIC VOICE AND POINT-OF-VIEW

Before you even consider submitting your work, you need to identify your authentic voice and unique point of view. You need to understand and be able to express what makes you stand out from every other poet. Publishers, contest officials, and readers alike are looking for a fresh perspective—work that inspires them to think about something in a new or deeper way. They also look for original work that engages them on a personal level. Understanding your point of view will allow you to tap into a true and authentic voice. This in turn will help you write work that is all your own. By putting *you* into your poetry, you will gain a deeper understanding of the unique poetry that you can offer the world (and the judges). It can also help you to avoid writing clichéd poetry. For more details on finding and honing your unique voice, see Chapter 4.

PERFECT YOUR CRAFT

Be prepared to write, and write *a lot*. Working toward publication means treating your poetry as both an art and a skill that needs to be nurtured through practice. You will need to spend time in the act of writing, and work on your craft to produce poems that are error-free, evocative, and original. A slick and error-free piece of writing tells the publishers that you have taken the time to polish the piece for submission. On the other hand, a work that has mistakes in it makes it seem like you rushed your submission, or worse, that you don't really care about your work or the publication. For more on perfecting your craft, see Part 2.

IDENTIFY THE RIGHT PUBLICATION FOR YOU AND YOUR STYLE OF POETRY

If you write sonnets, it doesn't make any sense to submit to a publication that specializes in haiku, and vice versa. Two of the best places to find the right publications and competitions for your poetry are Duotrope.com and Submittable.com. *Duotrope* is a hub for thousands of competitions; literary magazines and zines; and other publishers such as journals and publishing houses. It also has a feature that allows you to connect with a literary agent. The site is curated by a team of former editors, so each of the listings has been deemed qualified as a reputable publisher. To use the site, all you have to do is create a profile and log in. There is a fee for long-term use, but a free trial is offered so that you can see if the site is a good fit for your publishing aspirations. *Submittable* lists poetry competitions from a wide range of magazines and journals, and you can create your own profile to save the competitions that interest you. There is no cost to use *Submittable*, but many competitions do charge an admission fee for submitting your work.

The Internet will become your best friend in finding the right publications and competitions for your poetry. You can use common search terms like "poetry competition"; "poetry submissions"; "creative writing competition"; and also enter your country or state to find local submission calls.

FOLLOW THE GUIDELINES

Each competition or call for submissions will have a specific set of guidelines, which will normally include items such as word count, entry format, submission dates, and rules about whether or not you can put your name on your submission or entry. The guidelines are there for a reason. Publishers and contest judges are going to use them to qualify each entry and select submissions. As many competitions and publications get hundreds of entries, the guidelines are a quick and easy way to reduce the number of works that make it to round two. If the guidelines say your entry must be one hundred words, and you write one hundred and three words, then it will not make it through the first round of assessment. Make sure that you read the guidelines carefully and follow them to the letter. Most poetry competitions will also have a set deadline for submissions. Mark the deadline in your phone or calendar and give yourself plenty of time to work on your submission. Don't leave it to the last minute, as this will likely affect the quality of your writing.

WRITE TO THE THEME

Does the competition, publication, or publishing house have a set theme for submissions? If the answer is yes, then this will be a nonnegotiable element of your submission. Publishers and judges use adherence to the theme as a quick way of sorting through submissions, so if you write a brilliant piece of poetry, but it doesn't fit the theme, you won't get through to the next phase. Sometimes it can be tempting to cobble together an old piece and try to make it fit the theme (especially if you can't find inspiration or haven't left yourself enough time), but this often doesn't work, as the piece is likely to read clumsily or may not fit the theme as well as it could have if it had been written specifically for the publication.

UNDERSTAND THE VOICE OF THE PUBLICATION

What sets the publication apart from others? Do they focus on micropoetry? Do they focus on themes of equality and diversity? Understanding the publication can help you write poems that will fit its editorial brief, and bring your submission that much closer to being accepted.

The easiest way to understand the publication and what the publishers are looking for is to read previous print or online issues and featured poems. If there is a poet who is featured often in a publication, look for patterns in his or her submissions. If you are entering a competition, read previous winning entries. Look for consistent themes, forms, and styles.

ASK QUESTIONS

In the process of reading through the guidelines you might have questions. These might include: how many entries can I submit? Will the judges accept work that has been published on a personal blog or social media account? What are the format and style requirements? If you aren't sure, it pays to ask. Many publications and contests will respond to questions prior to a deadline. Having a definitive response to your question can only help improve your writing, as you will be able to better tailor your submission to meet the contest's guidelines. The worst-case scenario is that they don't reply, and the best-case scenario is you get your questions answered and submit an even stronger entry for consideration. You really have nothing to lose.

PERSEVERANCE PAYS OFF

Over the last two years, our editorial team has rejected more than two thousand submissions to our digital publications and annual poetry competitions. Online, we have viewed more than 230,000 post submissions and have reposted or featured approximately 2,500 of those poems. We don't share these numbers to scare you. We share them so that you can be prepared to keep going in the face of adversity. Maybe you will get published your first time. Maybe you will get published on your second try. And maybe it will take a few more tries to get published. Don't lose heart! Ask for feedback from the publication or competition officials and work on improving your poetry by writing often, submitting to competitions regularly, and sharing your work with other poets or writers. There are always opportunities as long as you persevere!

SELF-PUBLISHING: THE ROAD (ONCE) LESS TRAVELED

Twenty years ago, self-publishing would have been an insurmountable hurdle for most poets. Although there were options to publish your own work, the end-to-end process of getting the book physically published was time-consuming and very expensive, and connecting with readers was almost impossible. Today, modern technology and the Internet have given poets and writers like you the tools to self-publish without ever needing to leave home. Gone are the days of having to negotiate with a printing press: online publishing services now provide everything from formatting, content templates, and content and line editing, to marketing, sales, and distribution support.

Self-publishing can be broken down into two types: hard copy and ebook. There are a number of popular self-publishing platforms that offer both hard copy and ebook publishing, including *Amazon*, *CreateSpace*, *Lulu*, *Nook Press*, *Smashwords*, and *Kobo Writing Life*. Most of these platforms will charge a flat fee for services that you use, and then charge for a percentage of your sales. Be sure to shop around for the option that best suits your budget before you commit.

The process for these platforms is largely the same: write and edit your work, upload it to the platform, create your cover art, set your pricing, hit the "publish" button, and cross your fingers!

Before self-publishing, thoroughly research the process. Your research should include finding answers to the following questions: are the platform's services within your budget? How easy are their tools to use and what support do they offer as you go through the process? How much reach do they have and how many customers visit their site? How much do they charge in royalties and how will they make payments to you? What formats do they publish in and how much will it cost if you wish to print some hard copies?

You will also need to make sure that your work is properly edited and your cover art created prior to uploading. This may be something you can have done for free by a friend or family member, or it may be a service that you will have to pay for. Be sure to think about this, and allow time for the editing process once you have finished your final draft. The wonderful thing about self-publishing is that you will have full creative control over the process and the final product. Remember that you will need to dedicate time to polishing the final product, and if you stumble, keep going. Having your very own book online, and in your hands, will be worth the effort!

CHAPTER 12
The #digitalpoets Toolkit

With hundreds of thousands of poems being posted online each day, sharing your poetry with a global audience has never been easier. *Instagram*, *Twitter*, *Facebook*, and dozens of other platforms are offering unpublished poets the chance to connect with others, and published poets a way to grow their connections with old and new readers.

You have something to say. You have words inside that are dying to get out, and you want to share your creations online with the world—but you aren't quite sure how to put it all together. Look no further! In this chapter, you'll find a quick starting guide for your digital publishing journey, and a case study to ensure that once you are online, you and your poems are protected from plagiarism or worse—having your account hacked or stolen.

STARTING OUT: SHARING ON SOCIAL MEDIA AND CREATING AN ONLINE PRESENCE

Baring your soul on social media can be a daunting prospect. Not only do you have to think about the words themselves, but also the best way to present those words so that you can engage other poets, writers, and readers. In this section, you'll find our how-to tips for setting up an attractive and engaging online poetry profile.

BE YOU

We've said it before, and we will say it again: it all begins with *you* and your poetic voice. The digital poetry accounts that gain a following and engage their readers are the ones that are written with an authentic voice. It is clear from their work that the poet knows who they are and what they represent, and this in turn creates a connection to the readers. Begin your journey by finding your authentic voice. For more, see Chapter 4.

CREATE A STYLE AND THEME

Popular poetry accounts make an impact by creating a consistent theme and signature style. Your account might focus on uplifting poetry, poems for women, poems that explore a journey through mental illness or addiction, or themes of lust and love. The theme can also be aesthetic: a style of font, a series of images, or even the length of the poems. Identify the theme that speaks to your personal style of writing and presentation, and embrace it.

For information on apps that you can use to post your poetry, please see the App and Platform Guide at the end of this book.

CONSIDER LENGTH AND READABILITY

Long works often struggle to translate well onto a single image or post, especially if the platform has a character or word limit. Also, consider that many people access social media sites on their phones; a lot of text crammed onto a small image is difficult and unenjoyable to read, so people may skip over your post. You can use captions in platforms like *Instagram* and *Facebook* to make lengthier works easy to read: take a snippet of the poem, such as the opening stanza, and place this on the background image, then write the full poem in the caption so that it hooks the reader, but is also readable.

POST CONSISTENTLY

You don't have to post every day, but you do have to post regularly. Posting regularly will help you build a following and give readers and other poets a sense of your writing style. It will also mean that your poems are featured in media feeds regularly. A good guide is to post at least one poem every other day, and try to post between seven p.m. and ten p.m., as this time period has a high number of users online. If you aren't posting every day, consider liking and commenting on a daily basis to continue to make connections with readers and other writers.

USE HASHTAGS

Hashtags are important, as they allow other users to sift through the millions of images online to find what they are looking for. You should use around ten hashtags per post (you can use up to thirty total), and they should largely consist of popular hashtags, such as: #poem #poetry #writer #lovepoem #teenpoets #poetryisnotdead #poetrycommunity #writerscommunity. You should change the hashtags that you use on a weekly basis so that the search algorithms used by social media platforms don't interpret your posts as spam and reduce the frequency with which they are shown in feeds. Also, consider creating your own unique hashtag. This might be your name, the name of your book if you have one, or something similar. You can then add this to each of your posts and include it in your profile so that your followers can find your work.

The hashtag for our book is #youpoetpoetrybook, so feel free to tag your work so we can connect and check out your poetry!

CREATE NETWORKS THROUGH CONNECTION

Creating networks with other poets is not only helpful for growing your online connections, it's also a great way to improve your writing skills and talk about your shared passion. Other poets will give you feedback, like your posts, and tag you in the many prompts and events available in the online writing community. To start building networks, simply follow some poetry accounts that interest you, like the poems that you connect with, and provide some thoughtful feedback. In time, your network will grow and you will find that others are just as happy to support and promote your work as you are. Don't, I repeat *don't*, be that person who will follow an account to gain a follower, and then unfollow them once they have followed you back. It's just rude.

Also remember: plagiarism is *never* acceptable. If you love a poem and want to share it, check that the owner is okay with you reposting his or her work, and *always* credit the author in your post.

PARTICIPATE IN WRITING PROMPTS, CHALLENGES, AND TAGS

Many accounts offer regular writing prompts. You will find more and more writing challenges as you adventure through the online poetry community. Most challenge hosts also provide support and feedback, which is a great way to have others review your work. These challenges will also inspire your work, challenge you to become a better poet, and increase your following.

SEND YOUR WORK TO ACCOUNTS THAT FEATURE OTHER POETS' WORK

There are hundreds of poetry accounts that focus on posting or retweeting the work of other poets. Many of these accounts have thousands of followers, so it is a free and easy way to gain exposure for your poetry. Submission methods vary, but the most common methods are direct message, adding the account's signature hashtag to your caption, and submitting via the account's website.

DON'T FOCUS ON THE NUMBERS; FOCUS ON BEING THE BEST POET THAT YOU CAN BE

If there is one thing that we encourage all new digital poets to do, it is to focus on the poetry and making quality connections, rather than gaining likes and followers. If you only base your success on how many people like a poem or follow you back, then at some point writing poetry is no longer going to be enjoyable. You will always be worried about how many likes a poem gets or who follows or unfollows you. This can be horribly stressful and can make your poetry a source of social anxiety rather than an empowering outlet for your creativity.

As the saying goes, "If you build it, they will come." If you focus on writing great work that expresses your unique point of view and connects with others, and you get involved in the community, the followers will come. They may not come in the hundreds of thousands, but you will create real connections that will enhance your poetry and your online experience. You may even make some good friends in the process. We certainly have.

CASE STUDY: PROTECTING YOURSELF ONLINE

Aishanee awoke on a cool morning in November 2016. She found that she had an automated message from *Instagram* telling her that she had successfully changed her password. She had been using her *Instagram* account, nicknamed the Ink Alcove, to post her poetry for almost a year and had more than five hundred followers. Alarmed, she quickly clicked on the *Instagram* app to find that she could no longer access her account, and that all of the poetry she had created and the connections she had made had been stolen.

Like thousands of others, Aishanee had lost her *Instagram* account to hackers. Unfortunately, hacking is not a new problem on *Instagram*, or on other social media sites, and there are many ways that your account can be hacked, from not logging out of a shared computer to losing your personal information via a phishing scam. Fortunately, there are some easy-to-follow security processes that you can put in place to prevent a hacker from getting your prized poetry and claiming your hard work as their own. *Instagram* and *Facebook* give the following advice for protecting your account:

- Pick a strong password. Use a combination of at least six numbers, letters, and punctuation marks. It should be different from other passwords you use elsewhere on the Internet.
- Change your password regularly, especially if you see a message from the social media provider asking you to do

so. Remember to only change your password on the website or in the app itself, and never email your password to yourself or others.

- Never give your password to someone you don't know.
- Make sure your email account is secure. Anyone who can read your email can probably also access your social media accounts. Change the passwords for all of your email accounts regularly and make sure that no two email passwords are the same.
- Log out of your social media sites when you use a computer or phone you share with other people. Don't check the "Remember Me" box when logging in from a public computer, as this will keep you logged in even after you close the browser window.
- Think before you authorize any third-party app, and revoke access to any app that you do not use or can't fully trust.

We also recommend taking the following steps:

- Turn on "Two Factor Authentication" in your *Instagram* settings. To do this, click on the three dots in the top right corner to access your options. Scroll down and select "Two Factor Authentication."
- Create an email address that you only use to create and access your social media profiles.
- Regularly check what you have liked, and look for comments and follows that you do not remember doing. This may indicate that someone else is accessing your account.
- Think very carefully about buying or boosting followers. Not only is it likely that you are buying bot accounts (fake

accounts set up to boost follower numbers), but these types of apps have been linked to numerous risks, including account hacking. If it seems too good to be true, it probably is. This practice can also get your account shadowbanned, where your posts will not show up in any of your followers' feeds or in hashtag searches. You can even end up with your account being deleted, as bot accounts and apps that sell bot accounts breach the terms of use of most social media platforms.

• Put your name on your work! Don't forget to include your account name, real name, or both, on your posts. If one of your poems is reposted it will always have your details on it. Please note, there is *nothing* you can do to stop someone from reposting your work. Not only can they use a repost app to do this, but they can also screenshot and post, or even manually rewrite your poem using an app. If you do find that your work has been plagiarized, be sure to report the post and contact the account holder to have it removed.

Now you know how to start your online poetry journey—and how to stay safe when you begin posting. It's time to share your work with the world. Good luck! We cannot wait to see where the words take you. Remember to check out our appendix on apps, social media platforms, and other great poetry resources.

APPENDIX: APP AND PLATFORM GUIDE

This section will provide you with a list of apps that will help you publish your work online. We have also included links to various publications that will help you submit your work and share it with a wide, and often global, audience.

#DIGITALPOET APPS

The following is a list of apps that you can download to your phone from your relevant app store. New apps are being created daily, so don't hesitate to try an app that isn't on our list. Remember that you don't have to spend money on apps to get great results, and always try the free version before you buy!

WORD DESIGN/FONT APPS

To create an image to post to your social media account, the quickest place to start is with a font app. The following font apps allow you to type your poem directly onto a background image on your phone. The app will save your poem in an image format to your phone's gallery and then you can post this directly to your social media account like any other photo:

- *Font Candy*
- *InstaQuote*
- *Textgram*
- *Fotor*
- *TextonPS* (or *Text on Photo*)
- *Phonto*
- *PhotoGrid*

Pro tip: for intricate and complex poems, such as concrete poems that have a special shape or images that you have edited yourself, you can create your posts in InDesign, Publisher, PowerPoint, and other design-based software. Then, you can save the poem to Cloud or Dropbox, download it to your phone, and post to your favorite social media platform.

FRAMES AND BORDERS

You can use the following apps to add a frame or border to your photos or images as part of your design aesthetic:

- *Pic Collage*
- *LiveCollage*
- *PicsArt*
- *Photo Editor Pro*

Borders can also be added using design software such as Publisher, PowerPoint, or Adobe. Many font apps, like the ones we mentioned earlier, will have the option to add a border as well.

STORY

Use one of the apps in this list to resize your posts or images to fit the 6:9 ratio of *Instagram* stories. This makes the story slick!

- *Repost*
- *No Crop Story*
- *No Crop*
- *Video Downloader Pro*
- *PhotoGrid*

BACKGROUND IMAGES

Photos, drawings, and illustrations can add an additional dimension to your work and create eye-catching posts. Some images will require an attribution, while others are within the public domain. Why should you include attributions? If the site you are using does not specifically state that it is attribution-free, then you must do everything you can to ensure that you give credit for the artwork to its creator, otherwise you can be sued for copyright infringement. Attributing work is also important because, like your own writing, the person who created it deserves to be recognized for the work that he or she has done.

Here are a few ways to create or source images for your work:

- Create your own backgrounds: If you have an eye for imagery, don't be afraid to use your own photos, drawings, or pictures as the backgrounds for your work.
- Unsplash.com: All images on this site are within the public domain, so you can use and manipulate images without having to credit them.
- Pixabay.com: All images on this site are also within the public domain, so you can use and manipulate images without having to credit them.
- WeHeartIt.com: This site is a mixture of attributable images and images within the public domain. As a rule, you should credit images back to the website.
- Pinterest.com: This site also has a mixture of attributable images and images within the public domain. To avoid any copyright issues, credit any images you use to the website.
- Other creatives: Another way to find unique images for your work is to collaborate with an artist. There are literally thousands of artists on *Instagram* and *Facebook* sharing everything from sketches to oil paintings. If you use artwork from an artist, *always* credit them, including giving a link to their account or website if they have one.
- In an app: Most font apps, including the ones listed in our "Word Design/Font Apps" section, come with a range of backgrounds that are within the public domain.

Once you have your image, simply open your font app and set it as the background.

CAPTIONS

You can't copy other people's captions on *Instagram* using cut and paste, as the platform won't allow it. Here are some apps you can use if you would like to quote from another poet's caption:

- *Repost Quick*
- *Quick Save*

REPOSTING OTHER POETS

Love what you have read? Get an app to correctly share the work. The following are easy-to-use reposting apps:

- *Repost*
- *Regram*

Pro tip: use the watermark feature, which comes with most apps and will show on the image your repost, to attribute the poem to its original author.

VIDEOS

Want to repost a video? These apps will do it for you.

- *Video Downloader Pro*
- *Repost*
- *PicPlayPost*

You can also upload videos yourself. Once you have edited a video, download it from your Cloud or Dropbox to your phone, then post it to your favorite platform.

PUBLICATION PLATFORMS

The following is a list of publications and online platforms that you can post your work to. There are a range of publications, from social media platforms to digital zines.

SOCIAL MEDIA PLATFORMS

These are free and publically available social media platforms that are commonly used to share poetry.

- *Instagram*: Instagram.com (app available)
- *Facebook*: Facebook.com (app available)
- *Twitter*: Twitter.com (app available)
- *Wattpad*: Wattpad.com
- *Mirakee*: app available from the *Google Play Store*

We strongly advise that you set up a separate account for your poetry that is independent of your personal account. This way, you will be able to create a consistent theme for your account that doesn't link to your day-to-day life. Although you can share these elements with your daily life followers as well, if you have work that you do not wish to share with people in your real world, a separate account can give you the space to express your creativity without worrying about judgment.

LISTINGS PLATFORMS

The following is a list of sites that compile publication opportunities.

- *Duotrope*: https://duotrope.com
- *Submittable*: www.submittable.com
- Community of Literary Magazines and Presses: www.clmp.org

POETRY MAGAZINES

The following is a list of poetry zines, magazines, and websites that publish the work of poets.

- *Her Heart Poetry*: www.herheartpoetry.com
- *Poets & Writers Magazine*: www.pw.org
- *The Scribbled Stories*: http://thescribbledstories.in
- *Spillwords*: www.spillwords.com
- *American Chordata*: https://americanchordata.org
- *The New Yorker*: www.newyorker.com
- *The Atlantic*: www.theatlantic.com
- *Harper's Magazine*: www.harpers.org
- *The New Republic*: www.tnr.com
- *Granta*: https://granta.com
- *Literal Latté*: www.literal-latte.com
- *Poetry Foundation*: www.poetryfoundation.org
- *The Paris Review*: www.theparisreview.org
- *The American Poetry Review*: http://aprweb.org
- *Rattle*: www.rattle.com
- *The Lyric*: www.thelyricmagazine.com
- *The HyperTexts*: www.thehypertexts.com
- *Angle*: www.anglepoetry.co.uk
- *The Hudson Review*: https://hudsonreview.com
- *Light*: https://lightpoetrymagazine.com
- *Measure Press*: www.measurepress.com/measure/
- *Anon*: www.anonpoetry.co.uk
- *The Barefoot Muse*: www.barefootmuse.com
- *Boston Poetry Magazine*: www.bostonpoetry.com
- *Contemporary Rhyme*: www.contemporaryrhyme.com

- *Expansive Poetry & Music Online*: www.expansivepoetryonline.com
- *Fringe Magazine*: http://fringemagazine.org
- *Imitation & Allusion*: http://imitationandallusion.com
- *Iron Horse Literary Review*: www.ironhorsereview.com
- *From Whispers to Roars*: www.fromwhisperstoroars.com
- *Linebreak*: https://linebreak.org
- *Literary Bohemian*: www.literarybohemian.com
- *The London Magazine*: www.thelondonmagazine.org
- *Lucid Rhythms*: www.lucidrhythms.com
- *Möbius, The Poetry Magazine*: http://mobiuspoetry.wordpress.com
- *The National Poetry Review*: www.nationalpoetryreview.com
- *Raven Chronicles*: www.ravenchronicles.org
- *River Styx*: www.riverstyx.org
- *Ruminate*: www.ruminatemagazine.com
- *The Same*: www.thesamepress.com
- *The Lifted Brow*: www.theliftedbrow.com

Please note there are many more independent poetry magazines online and in print.

SELF-PUBLISHING PLATFORMS

The following websites provide self-publishing tools to help you bring your poetry to print.

- *Kindle Direct Publishing*: kdp.amazom.com
- *Lulu*: www.lulu.com
- *Nook Press*: www.nookpress.com
- *Smashwords*: www.smashwords.com
- *Kobo Writing Life*: www.kobo.com/us/en/p/writinglife

ABOUT THE AUTHORS

Rayna Hutchison is an author and poet from Auckland, New Zealand. She is the founder of *Her Heart Poetry*, a global digital community, zine, and press. Her recent work has focused on the trials and tribulations of motherhood, and an exploration of being a woman in a digital age. She is a passionate supporter of new voices, young poets, and people new to the art of poetry.

Samuel Blake is an author and poet who makes his home on the Hawaiian Islands. He is editor-in-chief of *Her Heart Poetry* whose recent work focuses on ideals of harmony and selflessness, both in society and with the natural world. He is an altruistic supporter of the arts in every form, sustainable living, and poets with truth to share.

SPEAK YOUR TRUTH ——

SHARE YOUR VOICE ——

HER HEART POETRY

Share. Inspire. Provoke.

—— #YouPoetBook ——